D0435798

a gift for

_____

presented by

_____

EDITED BY ELISA MORGAN

mom,
you make
it all better

encouraging words from real moms

Revell

© 2008 by MOPS International

Published by Revell
a division of Baker Publishing Group
P.O. Box 6287, Grand Rapids, MI 49516-6287
www.revellbooks.com

Printed in China

Library of Congress Cataloging-in-Publication Data
Mom, you make it all better : encouraging words from real moms / Elisa Morgan, editor.
          p.   cm.
     ISBN 978-0-8007-1910-4 (cloth)
     1. Mothers—Prayers and devotions. I. Morgan, Elisa, 1955–
BV4847.M66 2008
306.874′3—dc22   2007029705

Contents

Introduction

We moms need continuous encouragement, inspiration, and insight as we raise our children in an ever-changing world. For more than thirty years, the heart of MOPS International (Mothers of Preschoolers) has been to provide that kind of encouragement to mothers. And this book aims to do the same with a compilation of thought-provoking messages from more than forty seasoned mothers.

So take time to sit back and read a message or two. Be encouraged by the affirmation you find here. And when you're finished, pass that encouragement on to a friend. These life-changing messages may make you cry or laugh, but most of all, they will encourage you to remember that mothering always matters.

1

Motherhood

My mother's love for me was so
great that I have worked hard to
justify it. ~ Marc Chagall

Kicking and Screaming

The honeymoon ended in the juice aisle of the grocery store. The social worker had warned that once our new foster daughter felt comfortable in the family, she would act out to test our love and commitment to her, but after several weeks of sweet compliance, I decided she was the exception to the rule. I was wrong.

All she wanted was one of those syrupy, sugary, contains-no-fruit-juice drinks in a kid-sized plastic bottle. When I denied her request and moved on down the aisle, she pitched her little body onto the ground, kicking and screaming. I'd never mothered a four-year-old before, so I thought I'd better follow the social worker's simple advice for handling tantrums: "Love unconditionally, but don't cave in." That meant I had to disregard my first plan (give her the drink as quickly as possible) and my second (hide out in frozen foods until the tantrum ended). Wishing the social worker had been a bit more specific, I scooped up my screaming daughter and told her I loved her but she couldn't have the drink. She screamed louder.

The grocery store manager came to my aid (or maybe he was trying to keep the other customers from fleeing), put my groceries in the cold room, and helped me to the car. A wise father of three whom I had never seen before in my life, he reassured me that if I let her know I loved my daughter without caving in, she would eventually stop screaming when she didn't get her way. She screamed louder. Back home, she kept screaming until she fell asleep in the cocoon of my arms, both of us worn out by her tantrum.

Explosions of kicking and screaming occurred frequently for several exhausting weeks after that, but then, almost as quickly as they started, the tantrums stopped as my daughter realized the security of unconditional, unswerving love.

Love unconditionally, but don't cave in. The results may not be immediate, but they will come. And you won't regret the extra effort.

~ Shelly Radic

Dear God, teach me to love my child
as you love.

Most of us become parents long
before we have stopped being
children. ~ Mignon McLaughlin

What Have My Children Given Me?

How do your children make you better?

That's a backwards question around Mother's Day, when we are showered with messages from our children, thanking us for all the ways we make them better. For the ways we imprint our love into their lives. (Or at least we wish we were showered with those messages.)

But how about the ways children imprint our lives and make us better? This Mother's Day, I'm thankful for the ways my children . . .

Humble me: Before I had children, my opinions were filled with *always* and *never*. "My children will *always* do what I say; they will *never* whine their way through the grocery store or appear in public with green stuff coming out of their noses. . . ." Three children and many years later, I have lots fewer mentions of *always* and *never* in my life.

Tenderize me: I not only love my own children, I love all children. I buy Girl Scout cookies from every child who knocks on my door, and I can't read the newspaper or listen to the news without aching for any child in need.

Make me more real: I can't get away with stretching the truth about who I am and who I am not. Ever since they started talking, my children have been my accountability partners. They repeat what I say (even when I wished they wouldn't), and they tell me the truth—about myself!

Teach me to trust Jesus: My children's lives are filled with so much I can't control. I've learned to do the best I can (which will never be perfect) and trust the rest to Jesus.

~ Carol Kuykendall

Dear God, thank you for making my children fountains of life and joy to those who encounter them (especially me).

*Just the other morning I caught
myself looking at my children for
the pure pleasure of it.*
~ Phyllis Theroux

What Comes Easy

Normally when moms share about their children, the topics revolve around the difficulties we have with child rearing. We can spend countless hours discussing potty training, naps, sibling rivalry, playgroups, preschools, and anything else that concerns our children. We will sit and console each other over our sleepless nights, spilled milk, car seat horror stories, or the always-popular "what happened when I went to the grocery store with my child" story. Now, of course we can all learn great parenting tips and survival hints from each other during these discussions, but what if we were to share something that came easy with our children? We were asked to do so a few years ago at a MOPS meeting.

Wow, something that came easy? We all had to think about that for a few moments. We weren't allowed to use our maternal bragging rights about how "sweet" or "polite" our children were, but rather we had to think about something they did that caused us very little hassle.

My son was about three when we did this exercise, and I really thought that *nothing* was easy with him. At this stage he would eat two meals—macaroni and cheese and peanut butter and jelly. And my son had (and still has) boundless energy and the ability to argue like a world-class attorney.

After listening to a few moms, it finally hit me. A few things *had* come easy with my son. He was never afraid of water. He took showers in a tub seat from the time he was very little. And he loved taking naps and going to bed at night. Yes, it is true; I had a toddler who liked to sleep and who liked water in his face. In the past, I had never focused on what had come easy. Instead I had found it easier to focus on the difficulties.

I left that meeting feeling a little lighter on my feet as a mom. Focusing on the positive traits of my son instead of dwelling on the daily struggles of being a mom allowed me to see my son in a new light. Even today, five years later, I remember the affirmation that small exercise gave me as a mom.

Mom, what comes easy for you with your child? Ask your friends the same question. It is a revealing and refreshing way to share about your children and encourage each other in this season of mothering.

~ Marcia Hall

Dear God, focus my child's eyes on the hope that is in you.

Parents must have a tender
heart, an inflexible will, and
the patience and faith of saints.
~ French saying

An Imperfect Reality

"You're a stupid-headed ninny!" Not exactly what
I wanted to hear from the backyard, where my two
children had been assigned to patio-cleaning detail.
Especially since they had been out there for all of three
minutes, giving me time to get up to my elbows in
the raw turkey I was preparing for dinner. Now I had

to wash my hands (and arms!) and march into the backyard to referee.

It had been an unusually stressful week. But to my own surprise, I calmly washed my hands, walked to the back door, and dealt with the issue without raising my voice or expressing my frustration. It took a few minutes to work through my children's raging emotions, but in the end I hadn't lost my temper, and the patio was cleared of leaves.

Later, back with my turkey, I realized that I had definitely experienced a breakthrough! Sometime over the past few years, I'd turned a corner with my personal expectations and learned to live comfortably with a reality that never seemed to quite meet my dreams. My house isn't perfectly picked up or decorated. My kids aren't thrilled to carry their part of the family load. And there are a lot of imperfects in my life.

But today I am thankful to have a home, messy or otherwise. I am happy to have children, even when they argue and provide me with the greatest daily challenges I've ever faced. I'm thankful that the reality of my life hasn't matched my dreams, because I greatly suspect that it's the daily disappointments that have allowed me to experience contentment.

~ Paula Brunswick

Dear God, each morning when my child's feet touch the floor, may they walk in your footsteps and lead her where you want her to go.

Children are likely to live up to
what you believe of them.
~ Lady Bird Johnson

Mommy, Will You Lick My Arm?

"Mommy, will you lick my arm?"

"No!" said the young mother as she settled her pig-tailed preschooler on a seat outside the coffee shop. She picked up a napkin and handed it to the little girl.

"You've got to draw the line somewhere," the mother added, noting my curious eyes watching from a table nearby.

I smiled in agreement. The young mother was right. Even though the little girl was still a preschooler, she was capable of wiping spilled chocolate off her own arm. Later, when the two prepared to leave the table, the mother leaned over and wiped chocolate off the smiling mouth between the pigtails, knowing her daughter wasn't yet capable of completely removing the chocolate mustache.

Knowing when to let a child do something herself and when to offer assistance requires constant adjustments in our mommy brains. It means pushing a child to do something without our help, maybe even letting her fail at times. It also means knowing when to say yes, offering assistance when a task is too difficult, or guiding and teaching until the task can be accomplished without parental assistance.

Have you recently said yes to a request that could have been accomplished without your intervention? As your child matures, remember to regularly make those brain adjustments that will allow you to know when it's time to say no.

~ Shelly Radic

Dear God, keep my child's walk blameless and pure (Prov. 28:18).

> The joys of parents are secret,
> and so are their griefs and fears:
> they cannot utter the one,
> nor will they utter the other.
> ~ Francis Bacon

A Mother's Mind

A road trip. It's a three-hour drive to my parents' house, to be traveled in the evening, so it's a time to relax. My husband will drive and my son will sleep. As I sit in the passenger's seat and begin to unwind, something strange happens. My mind doesn't drift off; my thoughts don't cease for a moment of silence. Suddenly my mind is filled with items I thought I left far behind: things I need to get from the store, things neglected on my to-do list at work, laundry left piled on the floor, and thank-you cards I never wrote. I begin to miss the days when an hour in the car meant time to just do nothing. Those days are long gone.

A mother's mind never seems to stop, not even in the peacefulness of a quiet car. There is always something to plan for or something to regret not having done. In a moment of panic, I long for years past when my mind could rest. Then as quickly as that moment comes, it's replaced by the sound of gentle breathing coming from behind me. I turn to see my son resting peacefully in his snug car seat, and I know that I have gladly turned in my restful mind for the most precious gift from God. I know that it's normal for moms to have their minds filled with random tasks left to be completed. But in the press of these thoughts, let us take time to be thankful for the responsibility that has been given to us.

~ Beth Flambures

Dear God, protect my child from whatever is easy and whatever works so that he might desire whatever is right.

Duty makes us do things well, but love makes us do them beautifully. ~ Phillips Brooks

The Sweetest Words

At almost three years old, Sarah was still barely speaking. She communicated with her big hazel eyes on the rare occasions she would look at me. She had just been taken from a scary home life and was now being cared for by me, a stranger and her new stepmother.

For nine months I mothered her while trying to make a connection, but I didn't know if I was getting through or not. Each of those nights I told her that I loved her as I tucked her into bed, but I never received a reply. Then one night, as I left her room and walked down the hall, I was surprised to hear her yelling from her bed.

I leaned in her doorway and heard the sweetest words: "I love you. I LOVE YOU!" Her once-vacant eyes began to sparkle as she spoke. She had said "I love you" for the first time in her entire life, and it was said to me.

Nothing could rival the satisfaction of knowing that the investment I was making in her life was completely changing it. A girl who was withdrawn and afraid just months before had now learned to love.

That night I held her and told her that I loved her too. Then I went to my husband and cried, realizing that raising her was no sacrifice—it was a privilege.

~ Susan Hitts

> *Dear God, make love my child's natural response to life.*

I looked at this tiny, perfect
creature and it was as though a
light switch had been turned on.
A great rush of love flooded out
of me. ~ Madeleine L'Engle

Why I Love Being a Mommy

It was one of "those days." I had to take my oldest to the doctor for a wrist X-ray, my five-year-old was fighting with her twelve-year-old sister, my four-year-old was overtired and cranky, the freezer seemed to be defrosting everything, and the laundry never got done. Then my husband called to say he'd be getting home late. Ugh! I just wanted him to walk through the door so I could say, "Tag, you're it!" Seeing me sitting amid the mountain of laundry, my son asked, "Why did you ever want to be a mother?" I felt so defeated.

That's when I did what every wise mommy does: I called my best friend. As I started to whine, she suggested that I make a "why I love being a mommy" list. She said she has one, and she constantly refers to it on "those days."

After all my darlings were finally in bed, I sat down and wrote my list:

Being part of bringing a new life into the world—just me and God

Holding those newborn babies and nursing them while they gaze adoringly into my eyes

Newborn-baby smell

Snuggling

Having an excuse to play and be childlike

Learning more about my Father God through my children

Hearing giggling, silly songs, and bad knock-knock jokes ring through the house

Celebrating milestones—first step, first word, first tooth, big kid pants, learning to read, when the light goes on in math

Seeing my children unified in a family team and knowing they love each other

The pride in my husband's eyes that these are his children

Watching my son work alongside his dad and seeing them enjoy each other's company

Unharnessed joy released daily in my home from irrepressible children

Looking at my adorable little girl growing into a lovely young woman

Bringing my children to Christ and praying with them

Learning new things with my children, whether it's
algebra or the name of a bird at the feeder

Grandma's delight at the love showered on her by
her grandchildren

Seeing the world through my children's eyes

Discovering the mystery of a new personality

The challenge of motherhood and how it pushes me
to need God every day

It felt so good to read over the wonderful parts of mothering. Do you have a "why I love being a mommy" list? Take some time to make one so on "those days" you can remind yourself of all the wonderful reasons you are a mom.

~ Barbara Vogelgesang

> *Dear God, thank you for the honor of
> being a mother and for the privilege
> of raising my children, even on "those
> days"!*

2

Growth

> It is not until you become a
> mother that your judgment
> slowly turns to compassion and
> understanding. ~ Erma Bombeck

Actions and Reactions

Well, it's official: I am the mother of a toddler. There
are certain events in our lives that reaffirm we are truly

in a new season. Early one January morning, I realized I had moved to a new season of mothering—toddlerhood. My husband and I were sleeping peacefully when our three-year-old walked into our bedroom and tugged at my hair, asking for a place in bed. I unconsciously lifted him onto the bed and placed him next to me. Minutes later he sat over me with a strange look on his face, and then it happened, the experience every mother deals with at some point—being thrown up on.

The strange part? Not the actions of my son, but my reaction to this new experience. Five years ago I would have screamed, cried, jumped up, or thrown up myself at even the idea of someone sharing their sickness with me in this fashion, but not that morning. No, I calmly laid

there talking to him as he finished his "episode." Sure, I could have grabbed him and run to the bathroom, but it would have been too late and would have added to the fear and confusion he was feeling over this experience.

So I lay there, covered in his sickness, without flinching. No, I am not crazy. I am a mother of a toddler, and these are the things we do. The amazing part is the reaction of comfort that can come from a person who didn't even know she had it in her.

And my husband? Well, he slept through the entire thing, not able to enjoy this fun experience. But of course, that is a different topic entirely.

Oh, the joys of motherhood.

~ Beth Flambures

Dear God, assure my child that you walk with him through each new season of life. Convince him that there is nowhere he can be that you have not already been.

Of all the rights of women, the
greatest is to be a mother.
~ Lin Yutang

Yep, I'm Smarter!

Good news! In the book *The Mommy Brain: How Motherhood Makes Us Smarter*, journalist Katherine Ellison provides research to substantiate what we moms have known all along. Sure we complain about not being able to remember where we put the car keys or about losing our grip on current events, but we all know this: we are smarter because we are moms.

One morning my son Drew and I sat on the front stoop listening for the bus that would transport him to our public preschool. "I think I hear it," I said. "Do you?"

Drew moved his ear up against mine and cupped his hands around our ears to see if he could hear what I heard. When you think about it, this is a good idea, because our ears hear a lot!

Think for a minute about all the sounds you notice and accurately translate, gearing your actions to them, that you never noticed before motherhood. You know instantly whether your child's crying is a "pay attention to me" cry or an "I'm hungry and tired" cry or a "that really hurt me and only you can make it better" cry. You may be sorting through files in a corner of the basement, but you still hear a small body bounce from bed to floor and scamper through the upstairs hallway—and you can judge how quickly you need to be up there to intercept him.

Your senses, your intuition, your management skills, your relationship skills—take a few minutes today to ponder all the ways you are smarter now that you are a mom.

~ Mary Beth Lagerborg

Dear God, may my child's love
"abound more and more in knowledge
and depth of insight, so that [he] may
be able to discern what is best and
may be pure and blameless until the
day of Christ" (Phil. 1:9–10).

The walks and talks we have with
our two-year-olds in red boots
have a great deal to do with the
values they will cherish as adults.
~ Edith Hunter

Timing

He didn't know I was watching him. My son knew the
pool was off-limits without my husband or me around.

But knowing our two-year-old the way we do, we didn't trust him to obey simply because of our words. We took the extra precautionary measure of installing a pool fence with a locked gate.

Yet my small son was determined not to let poles and mesh nets keep him from the desire of his heart, which was to reach the water. He kept pushing and pulling on the gate, but to no avail. Finally, he dragged his Little Tykes plastic slide up next to the fence, climbed to the top, and tried to pull his body up and over. He wanted in. He wanted in—now! In this situation, I was thrilled and thankful to watch him fail.

In watching my son, I realized that I, too, often want things my way—now. But I also realized that by not receiving what I wanted, many times I have been spared much hurt and pain. Had my son succeeded in climbing the fence, or if I had allowed him to go in through the gate—even though it may have been the desire of his heart—my son would have literally been in over his head.

What if I always receive the desires of my heart—now? I may not be ready and may "drown" too.

I am waiting for my son to grow up a little more and learn how to swim before I will ever allow him this desire. I am thankful that I, too, have been protected at times from my own desires, even when I thought I knew what was right for me. God cares for me as I care for my children, and his ways and timing are always best.

~ Angel Shahrestani

Dear God, give my child the understanding to know and the patience to wait for your perfect timing.

Sometimes the strength of
motherhood is greater than
natural laws.
~ Barbara Kingsolver

Motherhood by Surprise

While not exactly planned, our children were not what
I would call surprises either. Each was welcomed with
excitement and the anticipation of what a new blessing
would bring to our family. With five children spanning
ages five to thirteen, I was beginning to feel like I was
finally settling into the "mom groove" and becoming the
fun mom again—instead of the tired mom who couldn't
stay awake through the second half of a soccer game. I
was also enjoying the freedom that comes with having

older children—time alone and, yes, even dates with my husband.

Just before Christmas, something was going on with my body, and while I prayed for early menopause, my husband was thrilled at the thought of becoming a father again. When two little lines confirmed what I already knew, my heart sank. *Here we go again!* I thought.

Sleepless nights and endless diapers—we were starting all over.

Now that the shock has worn off, I am realizing that this new blessing is a chance to be a better mom this time around. More experience, more patience, maybe even a better sense of humor.

Instead of planning what would have been our first big family vacation to Disney World this fall, we are decorating a nursery, growing a bit larger, and maybe even growing closer as a family. Hmm . . . I just might enjoy this motherhood by surprise.

~ Athena Hall

Dear God, instill in my child a grateful heart for every unexpected blessing that you send his way!

Like mother, like daughter.
~ Sixteenth-century English proverb

Direction through Disappointment

Life is full of disappointments. Little disappointments such as not getting on the team we hoped for or getting into the class we wanted. Big disappointments such as not getting the job we wanted or the clean bill of health we prayed for, or our marriage not working out the way we planned. The Bible tells us in Proverbs 3:5–6 to trust God and to not rely on our own understanding. We are to acknowledge him, and he will direct our paths. Trusting God, even through the disappointments of life, gives him the opportunity to direct—and redirect—our lives.

Recently my ten-year-old daughter, Karri, was disappointed with the soccer team she was assigned to. Karri shed many tears over this situation, and, I'll confess, I shed some too as I watched her heart break and felt some of the perceived injustice of the system.

Being the older, wiser parents with perspective, Steve and I used this "little" disappointment to teach Karri principles that will help her handle bigger disappointments in life that are sure to come her way. We talked to her about how God loves her no matter what, how we love her no matter what, and how we still have each other. We told Karri all the things that parents say in these situations—that this experience may be an opportunity for her to make new friends and to grow leadership qualities.

Imagine our surprise when we learned that one of the parents on Karri's new team was a member of an admissions committee for a selective program that our older daughter, Kelli, was trying to get into. God chose to use a soccer team disappointment to work out his will in Kelli's life. Coincidence? I don't think so.

A couple of weeks ago, I was disappointed over a potential opportunity that didn't work out. As I was expressing my disappointment, Karri encouraged me: "Mom, God loves you no matter what, and Dad and I love you no matter what. We have each other, and that's what's important. God probably didn't want you to have that anyway." I had to smile as the lessons she had learned from her "little" disappointment were re-taught to me.

~ Janis Kugler

Dear God, help my child remember your faithfulness when the disappointments of life come her way.

God grant me the serenity
to accept the things I cannot
change, the courage to change
the things I can, and the
wisdom to know the difference.
~ Reinhold Niebuhr

Don't Fence Me In!

Have you ever taken one of those personality profiles? Those profiles give statements such as "Loud noises really bother me," and you have to choose how strongly you agree or disagree with the statement. The results tell you about your personality.

After taking an in-depth personality test a few months ago for a leadership position at my church, the results showed, among other things, that I am very relational but not very well organized. Well, this wasn't an epiphany for me. Anyone who walks into my office or my home probably could have figured that out!

I don't mean to criticize personality profiles, but sometimes it's easy for me to allow these types of test results as well as the opinions of others to sum up who I am and to stop me from trying things that I really want to do. Do you ever do that?

"I just don't have any close friends because I'm not very relational."

"I really would like to help out, but I can't be in charge of the bake sale. I'm not leader material!"

"No, I can't help with a social event for my small group because I'm just not an organized person."

This way of thinking isn't very helpful for growth as a woman, mom, and leader, and when I allow myself to begin thinking like this, I feel the corners of an invisible fence begin to close in around me. Among the things my profile didn't tell me but that I already know is that I am a little claustrophobic. And even with invisible rails, I don't like to be fenced in. I want to recognize my strengths and qualities, but I don't want to use them as an excuse for not growing. So I am determined to tear down this fence and move into a life where I can try new things—maybe even venturing into the world of *organization*!

~ Rachel Ryan

> *Dear God, give my child the strength*
> *to try new things and to step out*
> *of her comfort zone in following*
> *wherever you may lead.*

> The phrase "working mother" is
> redundant. ~ Jane Sellman

Who's the Boss?

Boss is a concept we've all experienced at some level. I remember my boss from the jewelry store where I worked after school calling customers to report the status of their watch repair. He was patient and fun most days. But around the Christmas holidays, he grew tense, and I found myself sweeping the stock room, taping down the corners of gift-wrapped boxes, and pasting on an ever-present smile just to stay away from his bad side. His "bossing" influenced my behavior.

Whether you're an at-home or away-from-home worker today, as a mom, the most important boss in your day is you. You're the one who sets your mothering hours and tasks and follows up on your commitments. Clocking in, clocking out, fulfilling your to-do list, managing multiple projects and needs—you're the boss over your mothering role. What kind of boss are you?

Are you empowering and supportive, offering encouragement to yourself when you're moving in the right direction? Or are you punitive and harsh, judging your every wrong move for where it could have been better? You might be a combination of these traits, patient in some areas, ruthless in others.

Think back over the bosses you've had in your work life. Who do you want to emulate as you take on the management of your mothering hours? Like it or not, you're the boss of your mothering days. Decide to be a good boss to yourself, and you'll discover that you'll be a better mom!

~ Elisa Morgan

Dear God, move my child to serve others in love.

A mother understands what a
child does not say.
~ Jewish proverb

The Look

Snip, snip, snip. My son watched in fascination as the hairstylist snipped off twelve inches of thick brown hair, shaping his big sister's waist-long hair into trendy, chin-length flips and layers. "Danie, I think your hair's kind of funny-looking now," he blurted out. Catching a glimpse of my face, he quickly added, "But I really like the way it looks on you."

Puzzled, my stylist asked him, "What do you mean, Dillon? That doesn't make sense."

With kidlike honesty, he replied, "After I said it was funny-looking, my mom gave me the look, so I knew I'd better think of something nice to say really quick."

The look. A visual cue from mom that says, "Make a better choice and make it right now." For a child, it's a stepping-stone between needing a full set of instructions from mom and making the right choice all on his own. For a mother, it's acknowledging that when a child has the tools and experience to self-correct, he needs the opportunity to do so on his own. It's moving a child toward the day when he must make the right choice without any verbal or visual mom cues at all.

~ Shelly Radic

Dear God, build in my child an uncompromising stand for his convictions.

The parents exist to teach the
child, but also they must learn
what the child has to teach
them, and the child has a
very great deal to teach them.
~ Arnold Bennett

Do You Process?

As my seventh grade son transferred into middle
school life, I decided he needed to attend our church's
middle school retreat. I brought him all the information
and sat down with him, knowing that he would be just
as excited as I was. Instead Josh opened his mouth, and
"I'll think about it" came out. I was astounded. Think about
it? What did he mean? Didn't he know that all the other

moms had already sent their checks in? Didn't he know that some of the boys had already put his name down as their roommate? What would the middle school pastor think of me as a mom if Josh didn't go? Great, now I had flunked being a "good" mom, because Josh wanted to "think about it"!

So I let him. About a week later, I strolled by Josh as he was reading and simply asked if he had thought any more about the retreat. He told me he was considering it. I didn't bring it up again until the day before the late-registration fee would kick in. This time I nonchalantly asked where he was in his thought process concerning the retreat. Very quickly and with lots of energy, he said, "I'll go!" At that moment, I was very proud of my son—not because he had chosen to go but because he had taken the time to process the situation and had come to his own decision.

How many times do I, as an adult, just spout out an answer without really thinking it through? How many times have I said yes to something and later regretted it, or said no and missed out simply because I didn't allow myself the time to sort through the details? Josh reminded me that it is OK to stop and think about a choice or decision and to process it. Maybe I haven't flunked at being a "good" mom after all.

~ Kari Glemaker

Dear God, entice my child to ask that it may be given, to seek that he may find, and to knock that the door may be opened (Matt. 7:7).

3

Family

The family. We were a strange
little band of characters
trudging through life sharing
diseases and toothpaste,
coveting one another's desserts,
hiding shampoo, borrowing
money, locking each other out
of our rooms, inflicting pain
and kissing to heal it in the
same instant, loving, laughing,

defending, and trying to figure
out the common thread that
bound us all together.
~ Erma Bombeck

In Our Family

I chose to nurse my children, and my philosophy was "on demand," which translated to "often." But as a new mom, I wasn't very confident, so parenting philosophies from my friends often caused me to question my choices. Was my on-demand philosophy better or worse than the philosophy of my friend, who kept her child on a schedule? Why did I need to compare my choices to hers anyway? In the first few months of mothering, I lacked confidence.

However, it quickly became apparent to me that nursing wasn't the only area where parenting philosophies differed. Other moms and families made different choices on discipline, eating, schedules, toys, and more in the first few years. As my children grew, the variations grew as well. Other moms and families allowed different movies, experiences, and freedoms.

Rather than comparing or judging the choices that different families made, I found myself relying on the phrase "In our family . . ."

In our family we eat dinner without watching TV.

In our family we don't call each other "stupid."

In our family we wear helmets when we ride our bikes.

In our family we sit and have a conversation with Grandma when we visit.

In our family . . .

As my children grew, they had more and more opportunities to see that other families had different rules, choices, patterns, and habits. As a mom, I tried not to waste time and energy justifying every choice, boundary, or rule but rather would fall back on the phrase "In our family . . ." It became a safe place for my children to land as they grew older.

~ Carla Foote

> *Dear Lord, please help my children*
> *to internalize the values they have*
> *learned in our family.*

Heirlooms we don't have in our
family. But stories we got.
~ Rose Chernin

Family Made by God

I received an email earlier this week from my son's birth mom. She was sharing the wonderful news about the birth of her second daughter. I called my son to the computer to show him the pictures of his new half sister, and he exclaimed, "Mom, who would have ever thought I would have two little half sisters? Wow!" I would have laughed at his charming comment, but I was crying tears of joy. I am so thankful for the gift of my son from his birth mother. She is forever a part of our family and our family story. And my son loves hearing about his birth family. It was wonderful to share with my son the addition to his family and ours.

Like my son, I was adopted as an infant, and just like him I was raised with full awareness of my adoption. This fact has caused more than a few chuckles in our household. One day when we were talking about how our family came to be, my son suddenly realized that my husband was the only one of us who was not adopted. He told me it was kind of weird that Dad wasn't adopted like we were—he thought it was funny.

I am not sure exactly how my husband felt about that tidbit.

My child has his own unique family story. It will become part of his children's stories one day. Our family is unique in the way it grew, but every family has a story describing the events that made them the family they are today. What's your story?

~ Marcia Hall

Dear God, help my child to understand his special and unique place in our family.

Part of the good part of being a
parent is a constant sense of déjà
vu. But some of what you have to
vu you never want to vu again.
~ Anna Quindlen

Great Expectations

Last summer there was a new addition to my family. Molly, my now-four-month-old Saint Bernard, came
home with us early in June. As with any new puppy, we
expected a lot of work, but we were pleasantly surprised
by her relatively calm nature and her immediate desire
to "do her business" outside.

For the first few weeks, we watched her like a hawk,
and every time she looked like she might have to go to

the bathroom, out the door she would go. As time wore on, we began to relax and allowed her more freedom to roam the house. Quite honestly, I was beginning to think I had found the "perfect" dog—well, except for that whole 150 pounds thing, but maybe the breeder was wrong about how much she would grow.

Then Molly hit what I like to call the "toddler-puppy stage"!

The tally for the number of messes I have had to clean up and the items she has destroyed continues to grow, some giving me a good laugh and some, well . . . making me want to banish her to the backyard *forever*. Maybe my expectations for her behavior were unrealistic for her age and stage.

As I think about it, I realize this isn't the only area of my life where my expectations are unrealistic. Can you relate? As my own personal challenge today, I am going to evaluate the expectations I have for myself and my family. Where needed, I am going to make some adjustments so that those I love can relax and be who they are in their season of life, without the pressure of unrealistic expectations.

~ Rachel Ryan

Dear God, may my child grasp the truth that while you tell him to be perfect as you are perfect (Matt. 5:48), your intention is not that he be instantly perfect but that he would desire to walk after you, in the direction of perfection.

65

One of the most delightful
things about having children
is experiencing the miracle of
their development, watching
the delight, innocence, and
expression as they capture the
newness in each experience, and
sharing in the laughter of their
play. ~ Anne K. Blocker

Twins!

From the day we found out we were expecting twins
until the day they were born, I remember thinking of
them as a unit. Soon after they were born, we discovered
that the two girls were indeed two unique individuals.

They were (and still are) as alike and as different as any siblings can be. They looked identical, and most people could not tell them apart, but their personalities were distinct. It was a surprise to me that they could be the same age and same developmental stage and yet have such different schedules, likes, and dislikes.

Of course, we as moms are often tempted to treat our children all the same. Won't that stop the "it's not fair" comments? However, each child comes into this world as a uniquely created being. It's a joy to recognize each child's character traits, communication styles, strengths, and weaknesses. Do you see the differences in your children? It takes time to do so, but it is well worth the effort. By recognizing these differences, we have the awesome privilege of encouraging them in ways that will touch their hearts.

The fun part of having twins is learning to see them as individuals. I believe that by keeping their identities separate, we have taught them to be independent and confident young ladies. Although they prefer doing things together, they are comfortable being apart as well. It is equally important that we give each of our children a sense of their uniqueness.

~ Chris Ulshoffer

Dear God, open my eyes to the unique gifts and qualities you have given my child.

> Families are mirrors. Looking at
> people who belong to us, we see
> the past, present, and future.
> We make discoveries about
> ourselves. ~ Gail Lumet Buckley

"Heir" Care

I remember summer mornings at the beach when my fingers nimbly arranged fine strands of my three little girls' hair into six neat French braids. The half hour spent braiding was well worth the effort, because loose, long, flowing hair becomes painfully tangled when little girls splash in waves and chase seagulls across the sand.

To keep my girls occupied during the braiding process, I fell into the habit of telling stories of my childhood. My daughters loved hearing about Mommy being chased down the street by a mean black dog, creating Barbie villages that stretched across an entire backyard, and the Christmas Eve when a tiny kitten threw up all over my new blue fur coat. Many mornings they requested to hear my "scar" stories—when I sliced my kneecap on the edge of a metal slide and ruined my first pair of white knee socks, or when I had to wait in a long line with other little kids and a mean nurse stabbed me in the arm with a giant needle.

Why were my daughters so fascinated by mundane stories of my 1960s childhood? I think it boggled their minds that Mommy was once a little girl like them. A little girl afraid of dogs, in love with Barbie, and grossed out by throw up. A little girl who scraped her knees and cried after shots.

During those early mornings of hair care, my childhood experiences wove together with those of my children, intricately intertwining our lives like the strands of hair in their neat French braids.

~ Shelly Radic

Dear God, may my child respect the wisdom of those older than she. May she sit at the feet of those who will lead her in your righteousness and truth.

The bond that links your true family is not one of blood, but of respect and joy in each other's life. ~ Richard Bach

Teamwork

My family and I love to dress alike. We may look silly, but as we go whooshing down the ski slopes in our matching yellow-and-black jackets, we joke that we are the Arnold Family Ski Team. For the Fourth of July, we run to the store that sells T-shirts with flags on them in adult and kid sizes so we can look coordinated at the parade. We know we're goofy, but for us, it's cool.

Like all families, sometimes we forget that we are all on the same team. When your sister has a soccer game and a piano recital on your birthday, it's hard to share your day. A single toy occasionally seems worth fighting over for hours. Being denied a privilege that a sibling enjoyed can be devastating. But all teams must work together. And understanding that people matter more than programs or possessions can be a big lesson to learn.

Sometimes being a part of a team isn't easy. They don't call it team*work* for nothing.

However, being on the same team also has its advantages. It means celebrating victories together, no matter how large or small. It means having someone

who will stand up for you no matter what. The appreciation of being part of a unified group is something I hope to instill in my children so they know they have their own cheering section no matter where they go.
~ Jill Arnold

Dear God, help my family to encourage one another and build each other up (1 Thess. 5:11).

73

> My mother was the making of
> me. She was so true and so sure
> of me, I felt that I had someone
> to live for—someone I must not
> disappoint. ~ Thomas Edison

The Stars

This past summer my family made our annual trek to the Upper Peninsula of Michigan. The kids always enjoy it because they get to stay up extra late, and we even have a tradition of eating just ice cream for dinner one night while we're there. Since there is so little development in this part of the country, at night you can see an amazing number of stars. This was the first year the kids really noticed the difference, and my son said to me, "Mommy, there's more than three stars in the sky!"

I thought about how this relates to my life. God has created such an amazing world and has given me such wonderful blessings in a family. But how often do I take these for granted or allow myself to get so bogged down in my day-to-day tasks that I don't take the time to focus on what is really important? I fail to notice the daily achievements of my children, those small triumphs like getting the Legos to fit together and then getting them apart, or making polka dots on paper, or even learning that it is not good to stick a Lite-Brite piece up your nose!

In this season of raising preschoolers, when we have extra demands placed on our time, it becomes harder to remember the significance of those little things that make life so special. So whether you happen to be like me and live in a city, or if you live out in the country, find the time to take a drive away from the lights and busyness of the world and look up. I guarantee you will be amazed!

~ Kim Cook

Dear God, open my child's eyes to see the wonder of all you have created.

One day your children should
be able to look back and say,
"My family was the one place
where I felt I could be myself—
and be loved for it."
~ Bill Hybels

Family Cheerleading

The cross-country meet at the high school was under way, and our entire family was there waiting for big brother Nick to run past the checkpoint. Nick, a freshman, decided to try his first sport. As all of the other runners passed, our two preschoolers patiently waited for their hero. Soon the other parents and spectators moved to the finish line, but these two little ones waited. Sarah began to chant, "We love you, Nick," and Alex joined in with, "We know you can do it."

When Nick crested the hill, he was in pain but kept on coming. He passed us at a slow jog, holding his side but looking determined to finish the race. Now the whole family was encouraging him with, "Keep going, Nick!" Libby, the sibling closest to Nick in age, ran to the finish line with the preschoolers in tow. There they renewed their cheering.

As Nick stumbled over the finish line, his brother and sisters cheered and hugged him as if he'd won the Boston Marathon. Tears streamed down my face, and I congratulated my son for sticking to it and finishing what he started. The coach didn't think he would finish. When he asked Nick why he kept running and didn't give up, Nick replied, "Because my family believes in me."

Be your family's cheerleader and allow them to cheer you on too. Celebrate the successes in your family's life no matter what place each person finishes. A family that supports each other is a winner every time.

~ Barbara Vogelgesang

> *Dear God, help my children to value each other not only as siblings but also as friends.*

To acquire knowledge, one must study; but to acquire wisdom, one must observe. ~ Marilyn vos Savant

Making Family

Last night we joined a young family from our church for dessert and celebrated their son's first birthday. After

Garrett smushed his special cake, dumped over the plate, and posed for several pictures, he went off to bed, and the rest of us chatted about families, marriage, work, life, and God. Pretty heavy topics for a first birthday party, but so important as this couple is defining who they are and how they are going to grow as a family.

My husband and I didn't have all the answers to their questions, but we have walked through twenty-five years of marriage together, including celebration and grief, job loss, extended family issues, and a whole mosaic of life experiences. At one point, we found ourselves in a hard place in our relationship and sought counseling to deal with expectations, communication, and how to love each other better. We don't offer a perfect family as an example, but we do offer a safe place to be honest, ask questions, and offer encouragement and hope.

I remember needing the same kind of encouragement in our own early parenting season, when we spent time with one particular family from our church. They weren't a perfect family either, but we saw firsthand how they dealt with sibling rivalry, family issues, disability, schooling, and many other issues. They gave us insights on how to be a family.

MOPS helps moms connect with other moms for this purpose. You encourage each other concerning how to deal with sleep deprivation, discipline, personal growth, and more. But connecting with another family who is a little bit further down the parenting path can also help you decide who you are going to be as a family. Whether these become formal mentoring relationships or informal glimpses into another's life, spending time with families in different parenting seasons enriches your own family experience.

~ Carla Foote

Dear God, help my child be devoted to those around him in brotherly love (Rom. 12:10).

4

Journey

There is an amazed curiosity in
every young mother. It is strangely
miraculous to see and to hold
a living being formed within
oneself and issued forth from
oneself. ~ Simone De Beauvoir

Expecting

Yesterday I was on the phone with a friend of mine
whose due date with her first child is quickly approach-

ing. As we talked, it was impossible to miss the tone of excitement and expectation in her voice as she spoke of this new life she and her husband are awaiting. She went into detail about the preparations they have made. Diapers are neatly stacked on the changing table, fluffy blankets lay draped over the rocking chair arm, and ladybugs and dragonflies adorn the walls of the baby's room. The dog has even been trained on how to walk alongside the jogging stroller. The anticipation was unmistakable.

No wonder they call it "expecting."

Later on last night, as I thought of my friend and our conversation, I couldn't help but think of how wonderful it is that, as mothers, we each go through a period of expectation, keeping us excited about what is to come. In pregnancy, we are expectant about when our baby will arrive. Whose nose will he have? Will she be healthy? Will I ever get to hold him after my in-laws show up?

However, it doesn't stop there; we continue to experience times of expectation as our children get older. What will her favorite food be? Will he like football? Will she be a safe driver? Will he be a doctor when he grows up? These times remind us that God has wonderful plans for each one of our children and for us.

My friend thought that her time of expecting would soon be over, but I know she will soon find out that the journey of motherhood is more like a choose-your-own-adventure novel than a fairy-tale story in which the ending is always known. And even though we sometimes wish to know the ending from the start, it is in the mystery and suspense that we truly experience motherhood to the fullest.

~ Jessica Potter

Dear God, move my child to commit to you all that he does, that his plans might succeed (Prov. 16:3).

There is no friendship, no love, like that of the mother for the child. ~ Henry Ward Beecher

Diagnose the Problem

After my son had his fifteen-month shots, we took advantage of a nice day to go to the park, play on the playground, and have lunch before going home for a nap. When we got home, he was asleep, so I just moved him into his crib for his nap.

After naptime I noticed that he was walking funny, and I assumed that his leg was sore where he'd had his shot. All afternoon and evening he kept walking funny, but he wasn't particularly fussy, and we made it to bedtime. As I was getting him changed for bed, I took off his shoes, and out poured a whole pile of pea gravel from the playground. He had been walking funny because his feet hurt from the gravel!

Of course I felt like a terrible mom, but I also had to laugh. How quickly we can come to the wrong conclusions when we try to evaluate and diagnose what is going on with our children. My son had had a shot in his leg, which I assumed was the reason he was walking funny. I never even thought to look in his shoes.

As moms, we are often looking for clues as to what is going on with our children:

Is my baby fussy because I had spicy food before I nursed?

Is the sore throat strep?

What is the source of that angry outburst?

My incorrect diagnosis of my son's stiff-legged walk reminded me to not move too quickly to a conclusion.

I also learned a valuable little tip for a first-time mom on the playground: empty those shoes right away! A fifteen-month-old can't say, "Mommy, my feet hurt."

~ Carla Foote

*Dear God, help me to grow in you
and in my role as a mother.*

It's easy to complain about our
children. But when we want to
express our joy, our love, the
words elude us. The feelings are
almost so sacred they defy speech.
~ Joan McIntosh

Diary of a Kid Vacation

Day One: Today my in-laws took my children
back with them to Texas for a week and a half.
Whoopee! Party! I don't know what I'm going
to do with myself—I haven't had freedom like

this in over thirteen years! I can do anything I want. . . .

Day Two: I think I may have forgotten how to party. Let's see, I can go to the movies, out to dinner with dear hubby. . . . What else is out there? I haven't done anything on my own or outside the acceptable realm of "family activities" in so long that I'm not quite sure what to do with myself.

Day Three: Boy, it sure is quiet around here. This is a good break for me and my kids, but I really kind of miss them. A whole week and a half? That seems so long!

Day Four: Talked to the kids on the phone today—they've gone swimming every day, and Nana took Stacey shopping for some fun summer clothes. Abbey is learning to sew, and Becca is enjoying playing games with Peepaw. They say they really miss me, though. I really miss them too. (Abbey told me that her dad and I are "cool parents."

We've never heard that before—I guess Nana and Peepaw's "old school" way of doing things is just too different for my kiddos!)

Day Five: I don't think I can take much more of this. The silence is deafening, and I need hugs!

Days Six through Eight: I'm really bored—and really lonely!

Day Nine: Whoopee! Today I leave for Texas to go get my girls and bring them home. I can hardly wait! Party!

It was wonderful to get a break from my life as a busy mom. But no matter how much I thought my kids drove me crazy, I discovered I didn't like to live without

them. The first couple of days were nice, but the rest of the time my heart ached to have my children home. In the end, I wanted my hugs. I wanted my kids. I wanted to be Mom.

~ Susie Sims

> *Dear God, help my children to*
> *appreciate the heritage that is*
> *theirs in our family. May our family*
> *foundations be a firm reassurance*
> *for them as they face the questions*
> *of life.*

There never was a woman like
her. She was gentle as a dove
and brave as a lioness. . . . The
memory of my mother and her

teachings were, after all, the
only capital I had to start life
with, and on that capital I have
made my way. ~ Andrew Jackson

Unfinished Projects

Before I became a mother, I rarely left a project unfinished.

The dirty laundry began and ended its odyssey to cleanliness within a span of only two hours weekly, and that included the driving time to and from the Laundromat.

Dirty dishes? There was no such thing. After all, when one uses paper plates, the only time needed is for the trip to the garbage can.

Craft projects? Before children, I could routinely start and finish a sizable cross-stitch project in a few short weeks.

Those areas of my life are now dramatically different. An entire day can be devoted to laundry. Even then, the job is never finished. The dirty-dish side of the sink is continually reproducing more and more dirty dishes. My last completed craft project was a necklace, which was composed of cut-up green, purple, and pink drinking straw pieces strung on some yarn.

However, there are still three very important unfinished projects at my house that I work on every day. Emily is eleven, Julia is seven, and Michael is five. These three endeavors will never be finished.

Some days are extremely frustrating, as if someone had unraveled what I did while I was looking away. Parts of these projects I thought had been completed suddenly need more effort. Lessons I have learned as a mother sometimes need to be revisited and relearned.

However, one day these little "projects" we call children won't need the same kind of physically draining attention. The lessons that we are patiently and persistently teaching them will grip their hearts and not be undone.

~ Lisa L. Knoll

Dear God, thank you for the blessing of my child!

Parenthood is quite a long word.
I expect it contains the rest of
my life. ~ Karen Scott Boates

The Journey of Motherhood

My girls are ten years apart. That was God's plan—not ours.

As a result, sometimes I feel like I have a split personality. I've spent my life in two different worlds. After reading Berenstain Bears to one daughter, I would proofread college prep papers for the other. I have cheered as one daughter played bunchball soccer and the other played competitive high school soccer. I helped one daughter put on "a little makeup" for her first dance recital as the other prepared for prom.

Six weeks ago, I stood in awe as one daughter put on her first pair of high heels and the other daughter stepped into her wedding dress.

Perspective. That's what having daughters ten years apart has taught me. It has helped me understand that no one season of mothering is better than another—just different. Every season has challenges and joys. Yes, you'll be physically exhausted with little ones, but you'll be emotionally exhausted with older ones. Yes, you'll clap at the first baby steps, and you'll celebrate as your daughter walks down the aisle.

This is a good season of mothering for me. I know it is for you too.

~ Janis Kugler

Dear God, help me appreciate every season of mothering with new eyes that see life from the fresh perspective of my child.

"Walk the walk" matters. Children learn what they live. They learn from what they see and hear their parents do—how parents make things work, how they solve problems, what behavior is acceptable or not, what types of cues and words

win positive responses. Parents
can and do mentor through
their everyday actions and words.
~ Craig and Sharon Ramey

Mom Influence

I don't know how other moms look at their children,
but I was still seeing mine as a bunch of exuberant,
silly little kids until recently. My oldest son, who is now
thirteen, has begun working on his Eagle Award for Boy
Scouts. I spent some time with him at a scout event and
saw how the younger boys looked to him for approval
and direction. The older scouts respected his opinion
and easily gave him responsibility. He knew when to
seek counsel on decisions and which incidents he could
just deal with.

It dawned on me that this boy/man with a sometimes squeaky, sometimes deep voice was a leader.

Wow! As I watched him direct a small army of boys setting up camp, I wondered what influenced his development from the little guy who loved to give his mom sticky kisses and needed a night-light to the young man I saw before me. When I asked him how he learned to be a leader, he said, "By watching the woman who's led me all my life—you!"

I had never really thought about mothering as a leadership position. Yet a leader is someone who has influence over others, and a mom definitely fits that definition. That revelation has made me more aware of how I lead my children, since I still have many years to continue teaching them. It has also made me realize that I was chosen by God to lead these children, and I need to depend on his direction in order to do a good job.

Oh, and by the way, my son doesn't need the night-light any more, but I still make sure I get the kisses.

~ Barbara Vogelgesang

Dear God, help me be an influence for you in the lives of my children, a beacon pointing them to your saving grace.

The Mother-Daughter Connection

This morning I had the job of rummaging through my daughter Lindsey's baby pictures to find one for her upcoming after-prom event. On my way to work, I stopped at her high school to drop off the picture, her after-prom T-shirt money, an after-prom donation, and the payment for her graduation announcements, cap, and gown. Today I realized that my baby girl is almost grown up!

Actually, this reality has been hitting me quite hard for the past few months. This year has been filled with "senior moments" but few precious ones just for mom and daughter. So, as the time for leaving the nest is drawing near, last month I arranged for us to take a mother-daughter spring break trip, to make memories that I

hope will last a lifetime. As I reflect on the time we spent together, I can't help thinking back over the last eighteen years and wondering if I have instilled in Lindsey other memories that will come to her at the needed moments in her adult life:

Physical growth memories—Have I instilled in Lindsey that she is a beautiful woman both inside and out? Does she know how precious she is to her family, friends, and God?

Spiritual growth memories—Have I provided the spiritual guidance to my daughter that will prompt her to seek help from Jesus in a conflict, problem, or crisis?

Sexual purity—Have I shown her the importance of sexual purity, loving her body, and saving it for the right man?

Confidence—Have I helped her grow confident and given her wings to fly on her own merit?

Communication—Have I communicated to her well enough for her to mirror good communication to others?

As a mom, I will always be there for Lindsey, but now she has to take the next steps—move out, go to college, get a job, and someday have a family of her own. I have to trust that the memories and the values she has learned from me will give her strength for her future and faith to rely on God as her constant companion.

Mothering—an awesome responsibility with awesome memories, from diapers to tassels and beyond! What we teach our children today will be the values that sustain them in their future.

~ Cyndi Bixler

> *Dear God, thank you that there is nowhere my child can go that you are not there still (Ps. 139:7–10).*

If we don't change, we don't grow.
If we don't grow, we are not really
living. ~ Gail Sheehy

Mother of the Groom

My oldest son, Danny, is getting married in a few days. We were thrilled when he and Tiffany announced their engagement and wedding plans a few months ago. All those years of praying for my son's future wife became a reality. But when the news really sunk in, I began to realize that when my son married, I would be a mother-in-law. What would that look like? What was expected of me, both for this wedding and for the rest of their lives?

I went online to see what I needed to do to prepare for the wedding. After reading through pages of instructions on what I should and should not do as the mother of the groom, I decided to scrap the research. Instead I talked to friends who had lived through and even enjoyed their children's weddings and subsequent lives. Their simple wisdom offered me more peace than any website article could. They said to enjoy the sentimental wedding, to give advice only when asked, and to love and pray for Danny and Tiffany as they begin a life together as husband and wife.

I'm still Danny's mom, and I always will be. But this season of mothering is different, just as being the mother of a high schooler was different than being the

mother of a single adult, and being the mother of a pre-schooler was different than being the mother of a grade schooler. Like it or not, our children keep growing up, and our roles in their lives keep changing. Yet (whether they like it or not) I am always Mom.

I look forward to experiencing this new season and to being a mother-in-law to a beautiful new daughter. I will enjoy the wedding, give advice only when asked, and whisper this loving prayer for them on their special day: "From this day forward and forever, keep God's love within your hearts." Just as I will keep them both in my heart.

~ Amy Gullion

Dear God, prepare my children
for their future spouses, and their
spouses for them. Be working in their
lives even today while they are young.

Parenting is a partnership with
God. You are not modeling
iron nor chiseling marble;
you are working with the
Creator of the universe in
shaping human character and
determining destiny.
~ Ruth Vaughn

Mommy Watching

I like to mommy watch. At the mall. At MOPS meetings. At church or in restaurants. Why? Because I'm fascinated with the creative skills moms instinctively use with their children.

Take the mom I watched recently as I stood in a long line at the Department of Motor Vehicles (a necessary visit that ranks right up there with getting a root canal or weighing in at my annual visit to the gynecologist).

I passed my time watching this mommy deal with her preschooler as they waited too.

"What shall we do?" she asked. (Interactive listening.)

"Play," he answered.

"Great idea!" (Positive reinforcement.) "Let's play 'how much do I love you?'" This was followed by an obviously familiar routine of "higher than the sky, deeper than the ocean, wider than the whole wide world." Masterfully, she turned the waiting time into "I love you" time.

I've watched moms transform trips through the grocery store into hide-and-seek adventures, searching for the stuff on the list while skillfully negotiating the whine out of a child's voice. I've listened to moms' descriptions of how they hug those nasty growly bugs right out of their grumpy children and how they turn potty training into a game by using floating targets like Cheerios in the toilet.

Recently I read a job description that listed "accepting responsibility for achieving the best possible results from the resources available." The job described a CEO of a major company, but that skill describes what moms do every day! Moms are the best at creative problem solving, conflict resolution, motivational training, bringing out the good in others, multitasking, and delegating, to name just a few.

As I continue to mommy watch, I marvel at the God-given creativity and natural leadership skills that moms use as they carry out their eternally important job of shaping the future.

~ Carol Kuykendall

*Dear God, may my child so
internalize your acceptance of who
you've made her to be that she can
readily accept and encourage the
potential in others.*

5
Play

In every job that must be done,
there is an element of fun. You
find the fun and—*snap*—the
job's a game. ~ Mary Poppins

Resolution: FUN

One of my all-time favorite movies is *Mary Poppins*.
As a child, I dreamed of having a babysitter like her.
Mary Poppins kept order and had rules, but she made

it fun. She didn't forget that a spoonful of sugar helps the medicine go down. As long as the rules were obeyed, she encouraged and joined in childhood fantasy.

Mothering is the most challenging, rewarding, and fun job I have ever had. And that's quite a statement, considering I've performed as a clown with the Ringling Bros. Barnum & Bailey Circus. It's true, though—I love being a mom and the adventure each day brings. Sometimes I do feel exhausted and frustrated. Sometimes I just don't know how to handle a situation. That's when I need to remember to use some of Mary Poppins's ingenuity. I need to draw on my creativity and make things fun, not only for my children but for myself as well.

I've been known to draw faces on old socks and have my children use these puppets to help eat dust monsters. We've cleaned our wood floors by wrapping rags around our slippers and "skating" around the dining room. When a lost shoe needs to be found, I hire a four-year-old private detective. I'm more likely to enjoy cleaning the house if I put on some great music and pretend I'm doing a production number from a Broadway show.

Why not make a resolution to add more joy to your home? After all, a spoonful of sugar really does make the medicine go down in the most delightful way.

~ Barbara Vogelgesang

> Dear God, weed out of my child's
> life those qualities that are not from
> you. Plant the fruit of the Spirit in
> their place.

> A child does not thrive on what
> he is prevented from doing,
> but on what he actually does.
> ~ Marcelene Cox

Playing in the Rain

During a recent warm summer evening, I had an apparent lapse in my parenting judgment. At least, that's what some of the neighbors thought. I was outside with my husband and children when it began to rain.

"Can we stay outside and play, Mom?" they implored. They looked surprised when I offered an unexpected answer: "Sure."

My husband and I laughed as we watched our boys splash in giant puddles and run through the falling raindrops. One by one, neighbor children joined in, and all-out happy chaos ensued. What abandon!

When we finally came inside, two very happy and soggy little boys had enjoyed an unexpected frolic in the rain and made a wonderful memory, just because I said yes instead of no.

Don't let these dog days of parenting preschoolers bog you down. Have fun. Let loose. Say yes when you might ordinarily say no. There are some blissful memories just waiting to be made.

~ Jami English

> *Dear God, as the pace of life quickens,*
> *help my child and me to pause, relax,*
> *and rest.*

I do not want to die . . . until I
have faithfully made the most
of my talent and cultivated the
seed that was placed in me until
the last small twig has grown.
~ Kathe Kollwitz

Dream a Little Dream

When you were a child, what did you want to be
when you grew up? What kind of pretend games did
you play? I always wanted to be a mom. I remember
playing "house" with my neighbors and always being
the mommy.

When my oldest daughter was three years old, she
wanted to be a sweater princess. While I still don't know

what a sweater princess is or what she does, I admire her creativity!

My youngest daughter wants to be a teacher. Ever since she started preschool and had her first teacher, this has been the desire of her heart. Personally, I think it's because she wants to be the boss.

I still dream. I dream of being a champion ice skater (which isn't too likely at my age!) or of being a lawyer and standing in front of a jury, delivering a powerful closing statement. I also dream for my two precious daughters. Those dreams include their finding a profession that brings them joy each day, having loving people in their lives, having children (a long time from now), being self-sufficient, and loving God and knowing him as their best friend.

Dreaming is a good thing, because it helps us reach outside ourselves. I dream of growing old with my husband, seeing faraway places, and making new memories.

Maybe we're reaching for the impossible (like that figure skating thing!), but dreaming helps us see where we could go if we're daring enough to try. What are you dreaming of?

~ Susan Richardson

Dear God, help me to continue dreaming and to instill in my child the value of reaching for dreams that glorify you.

> Resist the usual.
> ~ Raymond Rubicam

Go-Go Boots and Rescue Helicopters

The temperature has finally caught up with the winter season. And with the cold come rain, dismally dreary days, and the perpetual look of twilight. My children and I are cooped up in our house and buckled down for what could be a very long week. My youngest is nursing a cold and is snuggled in my bed while my two older kiddos play "pretend" upstairs.

In this season of short days and cloud cover that never seems to let up, I notice that my outlook is as gray as the day outside. I cannot see past the sleepiness and darkness that come with sick babies and often-unpredictable weather. But the voices coming from our playroom are anything but dismal and dreary. They are filled with the sweetness that can come only from two best friends captivated by each other's imagination.

As my four-year-old and five-year-old explore the wonder of a new rescue helicopter outfitted with disco Polly Pocket pilots, I am reminded that these days are not about the things I had planned or my own limited capabilities. Instead these days remind me of the endless opportunities I have to see the wide-eyed wonder that happens when two worlds collide. Who would have thought a disco dancing queen, in her go-go boots and silver sequined bag,

would mesh so well inside the cockpit of *Animal Planet's* killer whale rescue helicopter?

I want to try to be more like my children: open to new ideas. They don't know go-go boots typically don't go hand-in hand with a whale rescue, so that doesn't stop them. How many times are we stopped by our own ideas of change simply because something has never been done a certain way before? In this new year, I will try to understand the difference between limited and limitless possibilities. Thank you, Ethan and Emma, for showing Mommy something new.

~ Dallas Louis

> *Dear God, protect my child from*
> *becoming afraid to try new things.*
> *Feed his imagination so that he is*
> *able to think outside the box.*

> I am thankful for laughter, except
> when milk comes out of my nose.
> ~ Woody Allen

Laugh at Yourself

Mom, when was the last time you laughed at yourself? I am not talking about mocking yourself or belittling the qualities that make you *you*. Rather, when was the last time you stopped to enjoy those qualities? Are you able to laugh at the silly things you do?

I do silly things all the time. That is part of what makes me tick. Recently, homebound due to a snowstorm, I started to get a bit antsy and decided to get a little blood flowing by cleaning the snow off my deck. Unfortunately, I don't own a snow shovel. (That is another silly story all in itself.) So I decided to use a dust pan for the job.

For over two hours, I used a small, plastic dust pan to clean off two feet of snow from my little deck. In the end, the deck looked great, but I'm sure my neighbors thought I was crazy. True, I could have waited a day or two and the snow all would have melted off, or I could have asked a neighbor to borrow a snow shovel, but instead I was a little resourceful (at least, that's what I like to call it!) and used what I had on hand. Isn't that what most mothers have to do? Looking back on it, I can honestly say it was a silly thing to do, a silly thing that brought me joy and continues to bring me joy as I think about it now.

Take a minute and think about something silly you have done recently. For some of you that may require thinking back ten minutes, while for others it may be a couple days. We all do silly things at some point, and I hope you can look at those things and find pleasure in them. Allow the silly things to teach you. (For example, I plan to buy a snow shovel this weekend.) But also allow them to offer you a special glimpse of who you are. Laugh at yourself and enjoy the silly qualities that make you *you*!

~ Rachel Ryan

> *Dear God, may my child find joy in who you made her to be.*

Tears suddenly come to a mother's
eyes when she watches her
children be happy!
~ Elizabeth Jolley

Out of the Box

Last weekend we picked up some new patio furniture. After we unpacked the furniture, we considered the wonderful play possibilities of the box. Our kids are in their teens, so they are past the play-in-a-box stage, but my husband loves toys and didn't want to see a great box just put out for the recycle truck. He started asking the neighbors with younger kids if they wanted a fun box. We were surprised when the family across the street turned us down. But my husband was undaunted and went further down the block to another family, who was more receptive to the fun possibilities.

At dinner that night, our kids reminisced about the fun box times they'd had in our basement and backyard with a variety of different boxes scavenged from offices, deliveries, or the alley. They even remembered the time when their eighty-year-old grandma crawled into the box to peek out the "drive-through" window. Boxes are good fun, and we hope that the next generation of kids on our block can enjoy making up their own games with imaginary houses, castles, or restaurants!

~ Carla Foote

Dear God, help me to relax enough in my mothering to enjoy the fun of childhood!

Some think it's holding on that makes one strong; sometimes it's letting go. ~ Sylvia Robinson

The Tent

One of my sons has always loved building blanket tents. Sometimes he builds them in his bedroom or the playroom. But most often he builds them in our living room. When he was young, I showed him how to drape big quilts and little baby blankets over chairs and coffee tables. I demonstrated the art of stacking books on a shelf to anchor the corners of the blankets. Then I helped him make his tent comfy inside with pillows, good books, toys, and a flashlight. Building blanket tents is a skill I developed when I was young, and it's fun to teach my boys this same great pastime.

There is a blanket tent in the corner of our living room right now. It has even more significance than those of past years. You see, my son is in school now, and he doesn't particularly like to read. However, since he built this blanket tent, he has been using it as his reading oasis. He also pulled some toys from his closet that he hadn't played with in years and stowed them in the tent.

Somehow the tent space has become a reason to do things he usually doesn't choose to do. There are no TVs or video games in the tent, so he chooses to read and play.

Does the tent match my living room decor? No. Does having the tent mean I can't move the recliner or reach books on the far shelf? Yes. Does it mean I have to laughingly invite any visitors to sit on the other side of the room? Yes.

But it's worth it. My son is using his creativity, and he's seeing that a change of scenery can give him a chance to change his habits. You know, I have been praying that I can help my boys find their talents and learn to enjoy using them. This blanket tent just may be an answer to prayer!

~ Sylvia Reese

> *Dear God, whatever my child does,*
> *may he do it with all his heart, as one*
> *who works for you and not for men*
> *(Col. 3:23).*

*Laughter is the sun that drives
winter from the human face.*
~ Victor Hugo

Laugh a Little!

Sometimes motherhood seems like such a serious job—after all, we moms are molding the future of the next generation. That's why I love it when my three boys help me remember to lighten up and laugh a little. And sometimes it's me we end up laughing about!

Just today, my second grader and I had a good belly laugh while heading home from school. We were thirsty and decided to get a cold drink from a nearby fast-food drive-through. As we sat in line, inching toward the ordering speaker, we busily chatted about his day at school. I love hearing all the details of what is going on in his life. In fact, we got so busy chatting that we never even noticed we had inched right past the ordering speaker and were heading toward the pick-up window—without an order to pick up! Once we realized this, giggles broke out, and my son told me, "Mommy, you can't do that!"

I sheepishly replied that we couldn't back up and were stuck moving forward. We laughed about how silly we must seem to the girl at the window, but we still got our cold drinks and headed home (still giggling). Laughter goes a long way in creating fun memories. So go ahead, mom—laugh a little!

~ Carla Dietz

Dear God, help my child find humor in situations, even when they don't work out according to his plans.

6

Memories

Like so many things one did
for children, it was absurd but
pleasing, and the pleasure came
from the anticipation of their
pleasure. ~ Mary Gordon

Making Memories

"Memories, like the corner of my mind. Misty water-
colored memories of the way we were." These lyrics from

"The Way We Were" flooded my mind this summer. You see, my baby just turned five last week (sniff). He goes to kindergarten tomorrow (sniff, sniff), and I've spent the entire summer trying to make memories. My husband thinks I'm crazy, and asks, "How do you *make memories*?"

Some days I've made those "I'm tired" kind of memories, the unpleasant ones. Like the day when I was angry about something and pushed the bathroom door open so hard that I made a hole in the bathroom wall. I just plastered and painted that "memory" last week. I remember the day that I had no patience and barked at my son all day long. I asked forgiveness for that "memory" by the end of the day.

However, I believe that my son and I have made some pleasant memories this summer too. Talking and reading together before naptime and bedtime. Serving others by taking food from a local grocery store to a food pantry. Camping out all night in the parking lot of a brand-new Chick-fil-A restaurant just so we could get fifty-two free meal coupons. These are my memories of his childhood, but I hope that some of these pleasant memories will be his too.

Through the bad days and the good days, God has entrusted my son to me for only a time. Letting him go to kindergarten is hard, but I am blessed with so many good memories. Just last year, my little guy told me that I looked the prettiest when I was in the kitchen fixing him pancakes. Maybe that's the memory I will think of tomorrow when he's eating lunch at school (sniff, sniff). Or maybe I can start planning the new "kindergarten" memories we can make together!

~ Miché Tentor

Dear God, fill my child's heart with good memories so that no matter where he goes, he will always feel the love that surrounds him.

Call it a clan, call it a network,
call it a tribe, call it a family.
Whatever you call it, whoever
you are, you need one.
~ Jane Howard

Road Trip

Beginning a few weeks ago, little bits and pieces of summer started cropping up all around me. Sticky popsicle sticks left on the sidewalk. A girl across the street running with eyes closed through a twirling sprinkler. The sound of flip-flops. The all-too-familiar melody of the ice cream truck making the neighborhood rounds.

When the signs of summer begin to show, my mind instantly goes to summer vacations. When I was a kid, vacations were always the highlight of the summer. Sandwiches in a cooler, car games in a tote, and a full minivan helped to create the unique setting for our journey. And unlike being at home with all of us involved in our own activities, we were stuck together for a whole week—like it or not—sharing the same car and hotel rooms and doing the same activities. There may have been some grumbling, but one thing was for sure: in the end, we all had fun, and our relationships grew as we learned more about each other.

So inevitably I begin to think about a vacation for my family. Where should we go? What do we want to do? Will we make it out alive in the end, being in the same car together for so long? The task seems daunting, but at the same time, I want to experience that unique closeness I felt with my parents and my sister when embarking on vacation, even if it means putting up with all of the other things that come with it—packing and unpacking, bringing the right snacks, taking turns listening to everyone's music choice, and keeping a glove box full of diversions. In the end, we may just have a bit of fun and come together even closer as a family.

~ Jessica Potter

> *Dear God, weave threads of loyalty, respect, and love between the members of my family. Bond my children in youth that they may enjoy each other in adulthood.*

> Very often we travel the world
> over in search of what we need
> and return home to find it.
> – George Moore

Saving Memories

I'm not a great scrapbook maker, but I admire those moms who are. Instead of a lineup of unique scrapbooks on our cabinet shelf, I have three large, clear plastic boxes, one for each of our children.

I purchased those lidded boxes many years ago when our children were babies, intending them to be temporary holding places for all the treasures I would soon put into

scrapbooks for each child. That was nearly twenty-five years ago. The children are now grown and the boxes are still on the shelf, filled to overflowing with all the keepsakes of childhood, from the newborn's plastic hospital ID bracelet to the dried flower petals from the prom corsages, and lots of pictures of life experiences in between.

Through the years, the kids have delighted in pulling their treasure boxes off the shelf to search through the contents for something or simply to sift through the memories. We've often pulled out pictures to make a poster for a birthday or celebrate a graduation.

Now that the house is quiet and the children are gone, I have more time to put together those special albums. Maybe I will. Then again, maybe I won't, because they still love their treasure boxes, which tells me that there's more than one way to save the memories.

~ Carol Kuykendall

Dear God, motivate my child to the potential that is within him. Move him to discover not just what is good but what is best.

A mother holds her children's hands for a while, but their hearts forever. ~ Anonymous

The Quilt

Recently at church, my daughter announced with pride that she, her sister, and I are making a crazy quilt using all of the girls' outgrown dresses. It's true! And this is not something I am teaching my daughters. Rather, this is a project we are learning to do together, each messy stitch at a time!

"Why go to all that trouble?" my friend Sue asked me. "I know a wonderful Mennonite woman who makes the most beautiful quilts. Just give her your girls' outgrown dresses, and she'll do all the work for you. The one she made for my daughter is perfect!"

How could I explain that the "perfect" quilt was not my goal, but rather a time to relive memories and create new ones with my daughters?

This quilt we are now working on has become quite a project. Getting it done is not the point. Enjoying the process is. We sit together each afternoon, cutting out

squares, talking about who wore this or that, and creating shapes to fit together in a somewhat tasteful way. The plaid of a first school uniform next to the calico of a first Easter dress may not be the best choice, but it pleases my youngsters. As needles fly, we talk. Both my daughters share dreams, silly stories, and secrets. It's girl time. Someday I will look at that quilt with two grown women, and we will see the perfection of the moments that drew us together.

I know that at times it seems easier to finish a project without the help of little hands, but the memories created during those times together are worth more than any "perfect" project could ever be.

~ Barbara Vogelgesang

> *Dear God, move my child to commit*
> *to you all that she does (Prov. 16:3)*

*I carry your heart with me. I carry
it in my heart. ~ E. E. Cummings*

Mommy for Life

A beam of sunlight was shining on the green carpet through the open door of my eighteen-year-old daughter's bedroom. As I entered her eerily quiet room and stood in the middle, I stared at her light green walls, now empty of all her posters. Dark smudges from her fingerprints and staple holes were all that remained. On the floor were some crumpled pieces of notebook paper from when she had cleaned out her desk and backpack.

This was all evidence that she had lived in the room. And that got me thinking—is there evidence within her of how her dad and I parented her?

Sweet, sad, and even difficult memories flooded my mind, each memory making our family unique from other families. I smiled as I remembered telling our daughter to turn down her loud music when it blared through her door. My emotions ranged from sadness and emptiness to joy as I anticipated her new stage in life.

Through my uncounted bear hugs, I have told her numerous times how special she is and how much I love her. Will she feel all my love and pride as she moves on to her new "season"? As moms, we leave evidence in our children's lives that will be with them forever. The responsibility of "mommy" is indeed a life-long journey.

~ Terri Kearney

> Dear God, help me raise up my child in the way she should go, so that when she is older she will not depart from it (Prov. 22:6).

*The precursor of the mirror is the
mother's face. ~ D. W. Winnicott*

Just Like Mom

A favorite story my mother relishes sharing with her clients is from my disagreeable days as a teenager. It's a tale of encouragement. My mom is a therapist, and she probably wishes she had been during my teenage years. Power struggles were common between us then. One day at the kitchen table, I told her, "Mom, you know that one day I'm going to end up just like you." That simple declaration gave her some solace that this time of our arguing would eventually pass. There was hope beyond the frustration of fighting with a teenager about curfews, friends, and homework.

As a mother of a preschooler, you will find that a day will come when "no" is not the answer to every request from your toddler. Green vegetables will one day be eaten without a tantrum, and getting your child bathed will not always require the speed and skill of a Navy SEAL operation.

Much to her surprise, my mom cried with sadness, not relief, the day she and my dad settled me into my college dorm room. I am grateful that the struggles we endured are now used to help other families who just need a little hope. Now it is with pride that I declare I ended up just like my mother.

~ Bethany Wingo

Dear God, help me be an example to my child and raise her up to follow you.

7

Choices

My mother had a great deal of
trouble with me, but I think she
enjoyed it. · Mark Twain

Laugh or Lose It

Last winter I found myself under the weather and
in need of rest. However, I was an at-home mom caring for two healthy, energetic preschoolers who w

ready to take on the world. By afternoon, I was too tired to keep up with my one-year-old son and two-year-old daughter.

Thankfully, they had just begun playing in my daughter's child-safe bedroom. This looked like the perfect opportunity for me to take a little break. It was nice that the kids had chosen to play together quietly.

Quietly! They were playing *too* quietly—a huge clue for me to check on them. As I worked up the energy to go see what they were doing, my son rounded the corner, covered in white powder. My daughter followed, covered as well. They stood in front of me like a pair of powdery ghosts with only eyes and lips uncoated. Cautiously entering my daughter's room, I found an upside-down toy box next to her changing shelf. It had been used as a ladder to reach a full, extra-large box of corn starch. I now had two kids and one bedroom looking like the North Pole at Christmas.

As I looked at my little darlings, I knew I had only two choices: I could laugh or I could lose it. I decided to live life to the fullest and laugh. In fact, I even took pictures to forever remember this messy, beautiful, preschool mothering moment. As soon as the mini photo shoot was over, I began herding my powder bunnies toward the bathtub. Looking over my shoulder, I realized I had one other chore to handle, but I knew what to do. I shut the bedroom door and left the corn-starchy room for my husband to clean. Sometimes it's good for Daddy not to miss out on those magic moments of parenting!

~ Susan Hitts

Dear God, thank you for the creativity and imagination you have given my children, and help me to appreciate it even when it creates more work for me.

Fun is like the frosting on the
family cake. It makes family life
lots more yummy and enticing.
~ Carol Kuykendall

Reese's Restaurant

"What's for supper, Mom?" The age-old question. My answer? "Reese's Restaurant." This statement is met with smiles and comments like "Yea!" and "Goody!" Do your kids respond that way when you tell them you're having leftovers for supper? Because that's what Reese's Restaurant is!

Every so often, I pull our leftovers from a week's meals out of the fridge and write up a menu with all I have to offer. I take the menu to all the members of the family, and each person chooses what meal he or she would like to have. Then I put together each person's "order" on a plate, warm it up, and present it with a flourish! It's a nice way to deal with those piled-up leftovers. It also teaches my kids that we can use what we have creatively and not waste food.

I don't present Reese's Restaurant every time there is an overload of leftovers in the fridge; if I did, it would become too commonplace. I want to keep it special, so I choose to offer this dinner option once every few months. I can't even take credit for this fun idea. My mom came up with it when I was young, and I would cheer when I heard what supper was going to be that evening.

After all, it's fun for children to be able to make choices, especially when they are young and so many choices are made for them. It can also be a learning experience for them as they choose items from the various food groups the menu contains. They can see how to create a well-rounded meal. Three cheers for Reese's Restaurant! Three cheers for leftovers!

~ Sylvia Reese

Dear God, help my child to recognize
the importance of fun in family!

> I love these little people; and it is
> not a slight thing when they, who
> are so fresh from God, love us.
> ~ Charles Dickens

Love Is a Choice

Before I had kids, I never fathomed how much I could actually love someone. I may have loved my parents, loved my siblings, or even fallen in love with that special someone. But the love that poured from my soul when I first held that precious, sleeping baby could not be matched. I may have been scared, but I knew that I would love this little child no matter what.

As my journey in mothering continues, I've realized that often love is a choice. It's a decision, not a feeling. When my two-year-old throws a tantrum, my nine-year-old and eleven-year-old are fighting, and I am at the end of my rope, I don't feel so loving. But I know I still love them. When my feelings are hurt by a friend, I don't want to love. But I am called to love. When my husband doesn't tell me he loves me, my love for him continues.

Of course we, as mothers, love our children. They cannot begin to understand how loved they are. And you know what? God loves them too. Even more than we love them. How can that be? God sacrificed his Son so that we—each one of us—could become children of God.

So the next time you hear "Mommy, do you love me?" look your child in the eyes and say that you love him or her. Then repeat it, again and again. "I love you. I love you. I really love you."

~ Polly Benson

Dear God, help me love my friends and my enemies. Help me love them just as much as you love me. Show me how to choose to love all your children. Thank you for sacrificing your Son to show me how much I am loved (Eph. 3:18).

Only love can be divided
endlessly and still not diminish.
- Anne Morrow Lindbergh

Endearingly Different

My two younger daughters are both learning to drive the same way they learned to read—differently!

At four, Danie plunged into books with confidence, quickly memorizing basic sight words and guessing with wild abandon at words she'd never seen. Read-alouds with my youngest daughter were hysterical romps that often had no relation to the content of the story. She drives with the same confident abandon, swerving into parking spaces, peeling off the line at four-way stops, zooming along the freeway—never noticing her poor mother is nearly hysterical with fright.

Natalie approached books with cautious interest, carefully learning the sounds of each letter, experimenting with different combinations until each reading rule was firmly fixed in her mind and she could perfectly pronounce every word. Read-alouds with my middle daughter were filled with precisely enunciated words, each one matched to the other as she relished every paragraph of the unfolding story. She drives cautiously too, rotating the wheel hand over hand as she rounds a corner, looking eight ways before inching into an intersection, and traveling along side streets so slowly that I relish arriving anywhere at all.

Each girl has her own approach to life and learning. Both learned to read and read well. Both will soon master driving a car, enjoying the freedom and accepting the responsibilities of a driver's license. Each child is a uniquely created individual, mine to cherish and guide. Differently.

~ Shelly Radic

> *Dear God, thank you for the unique*
> *gifts you offer me through my child.*
> *Help me to recognize and appreciate*
> *each quirk and personality trait that*
> *is unique to her.*

*Perhaps parents would enjoy
their children more if they
stopped to realize the film of
childhood can never be run
through for a second showing.
~ Evelyn Nown*

Going, Going, Gone!

When my oldest daughter was about five, she decided to play house with her one-year-old sister. "I'll be the mommy," Robin said. "Bye, Sarah! I've got to go to a meeting!"

That comment sent an arrow straight to my heart. She was right! I was choosing to be involved in way too many optional activities and committees, some of which I didn't even want to do. I was going to church. I was going to women's group meetings. I was going to Bible studies. I was going, going, gone! At that moment,

I promised myself—and my daughters, indirectly—that I would slow down.

It took a lot of effort, but slowly I pared down my volunteer activities so that I could spend more time with my children. I still struggle with overcommitment. *No* isn't an easy word for me to say. But a friend told me something that helped: when we say no to something, we're opening the door for other people to say yes, and they may really benefit and enjoy themselves.

As we enter a new season full of activities, these are my guidelines to KISS (keep it simple, sister):

1. I make a list of all of my outside commitments and evaluate how I feel about each one. Do I find joy in each commitment, or do I dread it? Do I want to participate, or do I feel obligated?
2. I set a limit for the number of activities I want to pursue or the number of hours I am willing to commit.
3. I eliminate activities from the bottom of my list (those I feel pressured to do instead of those I want to do).
4. I stick to my limit. If a new activity comes up, I compare it to what I am already doing and consider whether doing it is worth dropping a current project.

~ Susan Richardson

Dear God, help me to model good choices in my parenting so that when my child is an adult, she, too, will know when to say yes and when to say no.

Do not throw away your
confidence; it will be richly
rewarded. ~ Hebrews 10:35

Courage

Courage. What a big word. How do I pass courage on
to my children? Do they see it in me as a mother, or do
they see the opposite—dis-courage-ment? I processed
these questions a few weeks ago when I took the kids
to a nearby lake for the weekend.

It was a beautiful, sunny day, and we finally had
the chance to get out in the ski boat for some fun in
the sun. I had tried water-skiing a couple times before
without much success, so I wasn't very anxious to try
again. But as I watched more experienced skiers take

their turns, I began to contemplate my courage level, or lack thereof.

Out of the blue, my ten-year-old son piped up that he wanted to try. Now, at his age, water-skiing's not so scary. I mean, he uses little skis, and he only falls a couple of feet. So without a second thought, Josh jumped into the water and waited for instructions from his teenage instructor. And he *almost* stood up on the skis before the muscles in his body gave out. He was so proud of his accomplishment.

Next thing I knew, my teenage daughter wanted to attempt "boarding"—something even harder than skiing. (She had already mastered skiing.) She almost made it up as well!

Well, their attempts gave this mom the confidence to try one more time. And guess what? I made it up on the skis on my second try, and it felt exhilarating!

When we finished, we headed back to shore, content with our accomplishments, satisfied that we had taken the risk of trying. My daughter even said to me, "I'm so proud of you, Mom." Wow, what words of encouragement!

Where did our courage come from that afternoon? I think we received it from one another. My relationship with my children comes from the exchanges and experiences we share with one another. It is not one-sided.

~ Cyndi Bixler

> *Dear God, make my child thirst for*
> *challenge more than comfort.*

> Begin with the end in mind.
> ~ Stephen Covey

"Parking" Meters

Now that summer is here, the atmosphere at our house has become more relaxed. In fact, today I even put our schedule in the hands of my boys by asking them what they wanted to do. They decided we should head for their favorite park. After everyone was fed and dressed and the car was packed with everything from sunscreen to juice boxes, we were off.

As soon as the car stopped, the boys took off running to the playground, and the baby and I settled down on a bench. It was then I noticed it—the mommy talk.

"Is that a Tommy Hilfiger bottle bag?"

"Whose child is that putting the sand down the slide?"

"Wow, that's a really cool stroller."

"You packed a balanced picnic lunch? Aren't you a good mom!"

I guess the mommy talk has always been there, but today it impacted me differently than it ever had before. I think the reason it never caught me off guard in the past is because I used to talk and think the same way. Yes, like these mothers at the park, using their mommy meters to rate each other, I, too, would judge other mothers on superficial terms. But today was different. Today I came to the park with a new perspective.

As mothers, we all want what's best for our children. But what really makes a good mother? Is it having the newest baby gadgets or being able to prepare perfectly balanced meals? I guess mothering would be easy to measure if those were the only criteria. Maybe that is why we tend to look at these superficial measurements. When we compartmentalize our tasks into tangible little packages, we are able to get warm fuzzies from our measurable successes.

But here is the lesson I have learned over the years: mothering is more than gadgets, good meals, and all of the other measurable criteria. Mothering has more to do with the immeasurables like love, integrity, forgiveness, honor, and time—those things that build character and long-lasting boundaries into our children's lives, those things that really matter.

How are you measuring your success as a mother? During this park season, I encourage you to turn off your "parking" meters and enjoy the time and lessons you are teaching your children each day.

~ Peggy Ployhar

> *Thank you, God, for providing me with another choice—to be able to mother for your glory instead of the approval of others.*

I was often bewildered by
the task of motherhood, that
precarious balance between total
surrender and totalitarianism.
~ J. Nozipo Maraire

Breakfast Choices

When my son was four, he liked to pick which bowl he would use for his morning cereal. I kept an assortment of bowls on a lower shelf that he could reach. One morning we had a relative staying with us, and she criticized my son's choice of bowl. Andrew had chosen the biggest plastic mixing bowl on the shelf for his breakfast cereal. While I didn't want to dishonor my relative, I said gently, "He can use that bowl if he wants to; it isn't really a problem. I won't fill it all the way up and waste cereal."

Giving our kids choices in small ways, such as which bowl to use for breakfast, may seem trivial. But by giving them some room to think and choose, we can set the stage for later choices in life. Also, it gives us practice as moms in not being too controlling. Sometimes it's tempting to make a big deal out of something that isn't. It doesn't really matter if my child eats breakfast out of a ten-ounce bowl or a one-hundred-ounce bowl. And why would I want to start fighting over things that don't really matter first thing in the morning!

~ Carla Foote

> *Dear God, help my child to choose this day whom he will serve. May he and his whole household serve you (Josh. 24:15).*

8

Friendship

> Puddles attract little feet just like
> a magnet attracts paper clips. It's
> a great thing to watch when it
> isn't your kid. ~ Bruce Howard

Janie

My family lives across the street from the Martins, a
retired couple with grandkids in another city. My three-

year-old, Ethan, has taken a fondness to Janie Martin. Whenever we go outside, he always looks across the street to see if Janie is out. If she is, he excitedly waves and hollers, "Hi, Janie!"

Last night, I needed to go to Janie's house to help her with her computer. When Ethan heard where I was going, he put on his shoes quickly (which *never* happens!) and said, "I'm going too!"

After working on the computer, Janie, Ethan, and I went downstairs. Ethan walked over to the beautiful glass coffee table held up by two ornate elephant figurines that had been brought back from a trip to Guam. The table was covered in beautiful candles and a floral arrangement. In the blink of an eye, Ethan knocked over the glass table, and flowers and candles flew everywhere. When we looked closer, we realized that both of the elephants were broken. Immediately I felt ill and fought to hold back the tears.

We took the next few minutes to put the table back together and collect the pieces that had broken off each of the elephants. Janie was so calm and gracious about the situation—much more than I was. She had been the one to immediately check Ethan to make sure he wasn't hurt, while I was worrying instead about the broken pieces.

Later that night Janie called me. She told me a story of when her son at an early age had ruined a friend's very expensive couch. Janie explained that the friend had ranted and raved, overreacting terribly. At that moment, Janie had vowed she would never react that way. Things are just things, and people are more important.

The lesson Janie taught me through her actions toward my son spoke right to my heart. Things are just things—they can be fixed or replaced. People and their feelings can't. Now I just need to remember that the next time Ethan breaks something of mine!

~ Jill Love

*Dear God, help my child learn early
that life is not defined by the things
that he has (Luke 12:15).*

What is a friend? I will tell you .
. . it is someone with whom you
dare to be yourself. ~ Frank Crane

Friends

Friends. We all want them, we all need them . . . but do we know how to have friends or how to be a friend? There was a time when I thought I could function without the help of friends. I tried to be a self-sufficient mom. Then I learned I was expecting twins. Our third and fourth children were on their way.

During a rough pregnancy, my being able to count on a friend was essential for getting through some days. Then the girls were born—seven and a half weeks early. They were in the intensive care nursery at the hospital, forty-five minutes from home, for a month. My husband and I had to find a balance between caring for our two older children and being with our two precious new daughters. It was during this time that I learned to really accept the help of friends.

My MOPS group filled our freezer with meals, took care of our children, cleaned our house, and prayed for us. With family close by and friends like this, I was encouraged and able to get through those days. One friend came to our house early every Tuesday morning to help feed the twins breakfast and get them dressed so we could all go to a community Bible study. Now that is true friendship!

I hope that through the example of my friends, I have learned to be a true friend. I also want to model friendship to my children so that they can learn to be good friends to others. Our family motto is "to have a friend, you need to be a friend."

~ Chris Ulshoffer

Dear God, thank you for friends.

Perhaps the greatest service that can be rendered to the country and to mankind is to bring up a family. ~ George Bernard Shaw

All My Ducks in a Row

I'm the kind of person who likes to get all her ducks in a row and keep them there. My "ducks," however, seem to have different ideas, constantly scattering and rearranging themselves. For some reason, I had the idea that it was my job as a mom to keep everything perfectly in sync. Have you ever felt that way?

My kids were one and three when I realized I needed expert help with staying organized and maintaining balance in my family's life. I decided to seek the advice of a mentor mom who seemed to have it all together. I was hoping for the perfect formula that would solve my challenges once and for all—maybe a new way to organize my home and calendar or a surefire way to evaluate new commitments. Instead this mom used the pendulum to describe her approach: a natural back-and-

forth rhythm, constantly changing as her children grew, as their commitments and independence evolved, and as she and her husband changed and developed as people. She challenged me to work at understanding the rhythm of my family—our personalities, our favorite activities, our strengths and weaknesses, our current seasons of life—rather than seeking a one-size-fits-all solution.

Her advice frustrated me at first, but over time it has served me well. I still think longingly about having all my ducks in a row, but I am learning to embrace the pendulum. As my family grows and our seasons and circumstances change, it is fun to be creative with new ways to manage my family. I don't panic when my ducks scatter, and sometimes I even leave them where they land.

~ Paula Brunswick

Dear God, thank you for the chaos that is my family. Use it to teach my children that even when they are not in control, you always are.

You can't stay in your corner of the forest waiting for others to come to you. You have to go to them sometimes. ~ A. A. Milne

Friendship Co-op

My busy little preschooler loved to play—but not by himself. He either wanted friends over to play with or he wanted me to play with. We had fun together, but there were other things I needed to get done for my family: grocery shopping, cleaning, cooking, laundry. I also needed to spend time on MOPS leadership planning and phone calls. How could I find time to do all these things and keep my preschooler happy?

A friend had the solution: we would do a child-care co-op. No money or bookkeeping involved. Four moms and our kids agreed to meet every Wednesday morning—once a month at each mom's house. Twice a month, two of the moms could do whatever they wanted while their children had fun with friends. Often there would be a special craft to do or a fun creative activity a mom had thought up.

The other two times a month, those two moms helped to watch the children, once at her own house with another mom helping, and once helping another mom at her house. This was great, because even though two of us moms were watching the children, we also got to talk with each other and relax some while the kids played. Time with a friend was just as important to put in my schedule as time at the grocery store or time with the vacuum cleaner! And those days when I had a few hours to myself to do whatever I wanted were times of actually getting to complete some tasks I had started.

Our co-op was a great way to give our children the gifts of fun and friendship while giving ourselves the gifts of time, friendship, and a sense of helping each other. Just what this busy mom needed!

~ Sylvia Reese

Dear God, teach my child the value of friendship. Always surround her with friends that challenge her to grow in her relationship with you.

> I have often thought what a
> melancholy world this would be
> without children—and what an
> inhuman world, without the aged.
> ~ Samuel Taylor Coleridge

Les and Olive

When we moved into our new home with three sons under the age of six, little did I know that the home's greatest asset wasn't the big backyard with play equipment the last family had left for us. It wasn't the wood floors or the spacious kitchen. The best, we soon learned, was our across-the-street neighbors, Les and Olive, who had been married for sixty years.

"Mr. Les," as our boys called him, was so clean that he washed the visors on his baseball caps. On autumn days after his lawn had been neatly raked, he would walk his yard, picking up individual stray leaves. It bothered me that while the view out our front windows was of their immaculate home, their view was of our weedy, big-wheel-littered front yard.

I learned, however, that we were just what the couple wanted. As my friend Mimi says, "To elderly people, young children smell like sunshine and dirt." I believe that Les gathered those leaves in hopes that any of us—especially the boys—would appear for conversation.

And the couple was a special gift to us as well. Les was there to advise me when my husband was out of town and the sewer backed up in the basement. And Les alerted us when four-year-old Drew climbed into the car in our driveway, put it in reverse, and rolled it across the street to Les's curb with the door open and his chubby leg hanging out.

Olive, or "Olub," as Drew called her, specialized in oatmeal cookies. And since it was just Les and Olive, they always needed help eating them! Les had a pool table in the basement where any one of the boys could play, on occasion, with their daddy and Mr. Les.

Some of us have parents nearby who are a Les and Olive for us and for our children. Some of us don't—even when our parents do live nearby. But most of us can find a Les and Olive in our neighborhood or church. Who in your life could be your Les and Olive? Enjoy them!

~ Mary Beth Lagerborg

Dear God, help my child recognize the wealth of knowledge and love that can be found in the older generations around us.

You're not famous until my mother
has heard of you. ~ Jay Leno

What's in a Name

I was in a hurry as I picked up my kindergartner from
school to take my two-year-old to a doctor's appoint-
ment. Headed toward the school office, I passed a lady
and, as an afterthought, greeted her with, "Hi, Linda." She
immediately stopped and turned around and, with a
puzzled expression, replied, "You called me by my name.
How did you know my name?" I stopped (forgetting that
I was in a hurry) and explained that I had met her a
couple years ago. She was surprised and instantly began
smiling. She told me no one ever remembers her name
and was so appreciative that I had. She asked my name

and said she isn't very good at remembering names, but she was so glad when others were. As she walked away, smiling, I realized how special I had made her feel just by speaking her name.

So many times I had passed her without saying anything, just keeping to myself. I realized just how significant saying someone's name can be. As I think about it more, I realize how much it means to me to hear other people call me by name—something about feeling included or liked or at least remembered—and it reminds me that I am an individual, not just Andrew's mom, Ethan's mommy, or Steve's wife.

It's just a little thing, someone's name. But my new goal is to be more deliberate in taking the time to acknowledge other moms and call them by name.

~ Jill Love

Dear God, give my child a heart full of compassion and love for those around her.

When someone allows you to bear
his burdens, you have found deep
friendship. ~ Anonymous

Opportunities

The email subject line reads "Opportunities." That's a
secret code from my friend. Translated in mommy lingo,
it means "Can you watch Emma?"

My three boys attend school now. I guess I could
say "been there, done that" and easily pile on the reasons *not* to babysit. But I accept and thank her for the
"opportunity."

Mostly I accept because I remember. I remember feeling guilty in asking others to watch my children. I remember wanting a haircut, a nap, a chance to be alone with

only one child, or lunch with grown-ups. Surely Emma's mom wants all these things too. Moms with young children need help, I recall, and now I could help.

But even in my new stage of mothering, I need help too. Juggling carpools mostly. And I need encouragement to stay the course with a teenager who can see over my head but not into the future.

There are moms further down the parenting road or walking with me who help. They pick up or drop off a boy . . . or two. They show me their grown sons' zigzaggy paths to responsible adulthood, laughing now about the bumpy ride and college bills.

My helper moms pitch in because *they* remember. Now it is their opportunity to be the one looking back with confidence earned from survival, knowing none of us will ever be done mothering or helping.

~ Erin Lehmann

> *Dear God, help my child be a friend*
> *who puts others before herself.*

A true friend is the gift of God,
and he only, who made hearts,
can unite them. ~ Robert South

Mom Friends

When I became a mom, many of my friendships changed. Don't misunderstand me; I remained close with friends from before becoming a mom, but I also entered a season with new "mom" friends.

You see, playdates aren't just for kids, they're for moms too. I have no problem driving forty five minutes to meet my sister so our kids can play while we visit. But one of the secret codes of mom friends is that you understand you're never 100 percent listening to each other, because part of you is always in tune with what is going on with the kids—whether it's playing referee, kissing owies, or losing your train of thought while your child crawls all over you, saying, "Mommy, Mommy, look at me!" *Hmm . . . what were we talking about?*

Mom friends pop up in the oddest places. I met a neighbor while on a walk one day. I called out to her, "How old is your son?" I didn't know her at all, but I knew she was a mom. Since then we've become good friends. Just getting our boys together so they can wear out each other instead of us is a great thing!

Honestly, I've had many encouraging talks with my friends among the fun chaos of motherhood. The value of mom friends comes from the mutual understanding of this season of life and knowing we are not alone.

~ Stephanie Rich

Dear God, bring friends into my child's life who can walk with him through the ups and downs that will come his way.

9

Obstacles

Teach your children to embrace
life as an experience filled
with endless possibilities
for positively affecting the
quality of their lives and
for transforming the world.
~ Steven Carr Reuben

Talk About a Bad Hair Day

March 28, 2005—a day that will live in infamy in my house. Just ask my boys. It was the day my hair fell out. You see, I'm a breast cancer survivor, and this story is one of how my boys helped me survive a difficult day.

It was the first day of spring break, and we were going to paint pottery. Before we could go, I needed to shower, but I knew that if I got my hair wet, there was a good chance it would fall out. Everyone warned me that approximately fifteen to twenty days after my first treatment, I would lose my hair. And I did. Massive chunks of hair. Nothing could have prepared me for this experience. I left the shower and brushed large chunks of hair off my head. I could only sit down and cry. I asked God, "Why now, while my boys are home? Why now?"

Hearing my tears, my boys asked through the door if I was OK. I replied no and warned them to be prepared for what I looked like. The boys knew what was happening to me. Jacob had even tried on my wig. But this day was tough for all of us. Jonathan looked at me like a deer in the headlights. Jacob began to cry, jumped in my lap, and hugged me the tightest I have ever been hugged. There was my answer. That is why God chose today. I needed that hug and support because God did not want me to be alone and feel sorry for myself.

Bravely Jonathan asked if we were still going to paint pottery. With that question, I knew God was giving me the opportunity, that very second, to show my boys what strength was all about. So instead of lying in bed all day and eating chocolate (which was very tempting), I got up and threw my hair and hairbrush in the trash. I got dressed and put on the wig, and off we went to paint pottery. I knew that God was walking through that time with me and that I would go on living because, as I discovered, my boys, my husband, and my friends were what mattered, and they loved me, not my hair.

~ Janice Joos

Dear God, in the dark times of my child's life, be his light. When there is winter all about him, breathe into his days your breath of spring.

There was never a child so lovely but his mother was glad to get him asleep. ~ Ralph Waldo Emerson

Wildfire!

It's fire season, a time many drought-suffering communities in the American West have come to dread. We collectively watch the horizon for smoke plumes, sniff the air for an acrid smell, and pray that the order to evacuate will not come our way.

While my city has been spared a major fire, some nearby areas have been devastated. Where once grew lush green forests, full of trees hundreds of years old, there are now moonscape-like wastelands. New plants have begun to grow almost immediately, but it will be generations before the forest is completely restored. What is sad, experts tell us, is that much of the severity is the result of human mismanagement—for decades the governmental policy has been to aggressively fight all fires and deny even small, nature-caused fires the opportunity to burn small areas and make the forest healthier.

The wildfires and the devastation they cause paint a vivid picture for me of uncontrolled, unhealthy anger. As a mom, I have struggled to consistently and appropriately deal with the temptation of anger. My children truly exasperate me sometimes, and more than once the wildfire of anger has blazed through my home.

A few summers ago, I made the connection between the fires outside and the fires in my own attitude and reactions. Suddenly, every time I began to "lose it," the picture of a burned-over mountain would flash in my mind. I began to see the potential impact of my wild-fire anger on my children: damage to their self-esteem, confusion, fear, helplessness, difficulty managing their own anger. . . . Ultimately, if I didn't try to control myself, I could cause damage that would truly take generations to overcome!

We all get angry and snap at our kids sometimes, and an occasional outburst will not ruin a child. But for me, there is no greater motivator for change than this picture of devastation, and many times this vivid mental image has stopped me cold and reminded me to take time to work through my anger before addressing my children. Even better, seeing anger as a wildfire has helped me recognize the importance of managing it well. I started taking consistent, daily steps to manage my emotions more productively in all areas of my life, making me a healthier person more prepared for the bigger fires.

This fire season, as I scan the horizon for smoke plumes, I will also scan my life for danger signals that I have become lax in my personal wildfire management. And I will pray that my home will never know the total devastation of a mother's anger burning out of control.

~ Paula Brunswick

Dear God, guard my child from a quick-tempered spirit. Teach her that rash decisions and words often lead to foolish results.

Before I got married I had six
theories about bringing up
children; now I have six children
and no theories. ~ John Wilmot

A Breath of Fresh Air

After a morning of running errands and making an overdue trip to the gym, I finally headed home to put groceries away and take a hot shower. As I struggled into my house with my grocery bags, I was surprised to find a tiny hummingbird frantically flying back and forth, trying to get outside. Just watching it flutter, chirp, and crash over and over made me feel stressed. Figuring it must need my help, I dropped everything to open the windows and doors. I tried nudging it along with our long duster, but that didn't help. After a few minutes of chasing the hummingbird across the house, I realized I was only frustrating myself by trying so hard. I stepped away for a few minutes and took a breath of fresh air, reminding myself that the hummingbird would find its own way to fly out when it was ready.

Have you ever felt this way as a mom? We sometimes get impatient when our little ones need extra time to struggle through potty training, dressing themselves, or learning to share. Lovingly we teach them, but frustration can set in when their learning takes longer than we think it should. By taking a deep breath and stepping back for a few minutes, we can refresh ourselves with new perspective and patience.

When getting dressed, my preschool boys often announced, "I do it myself!" Their outfits ranged from cowboy boots with plaid shorts and striped shirts to the occasional Batman cape over pajamas. Their clothing choices made me laugh and helped me realize what mattered most was that little by little, my children were learning and doing things in their own time.

As for the bird, when I returned from my break, my little friend zoomed past me and flew away . . . all by itself!

~ Carla Dietz

Dear God, help my child to grow and learn at just the pace you have set for him.

Play together and pray together.
~ Irish proverb

Empty

As the gas light came on in my car, I suddenly felt a close kinship to the gray vehicle. I had gotten to the point where I felt like a warning light must have come on in the middle of my forehead, proclaiming for the entire world to see that I was empty. Drained of patience. Depleted of emotional concern for those around me. Void of enthusiastic motivation. Empty.

I had watched my personal warning light blink off and on for the past few weeks, warning me that my tolerance level for those around me was getting dangerously low. But rather than making time to evaluate what was going on and finding ways to refill and refresh my spirit, I had continued with my busy schedule. Surely I could drown out any warning signs with the busyness of my week, right? Wrong.

And the blowout was not a pretty sight. What, you might be asking, was the tipping point that caused my angry tirade? I would love to tell you that it was over some important cause that would somehow slightly justify my actions. But the truth of the matter is, it was over the *arrangement* of cookies on a cookie sheet. And not even the hard-to-make, long-hours-spent-over cookies, but rather the kind you buy in the store and pop in the oven. Yes, it was bad.

So where do I go from here? I have made my apologies and moved on, but how can I guarantee the incident won't happen again? I can't. But I can watch for those early warning signs in my life and take time out to renew myself. For many moms, MOPS groups are a great source for renewal. I also find that spending some quiet time with God and talking through my frustrations with a close, trusted friend help refill my waning spirit. So whether you are just seeing the early warning signs or have already faced your own blowout, I encourage you to figure out what kind of "service plan" you need to keep your spirit renewed and full.

~ Rachel Ryan

> *Dear God, help me to model to my children that I must turn to you first when I am in need.*

> Children have never been very
> good at listening to their elders,
> but they have never failed to
> imitate them. ~ James Baldwin

Limitations

Summer and swimming go hand in hand where we live in Southern California. Therefore, I was happy to find that this summer's swim lessons proved successful for my youngest son, four-year-old Darius—to a certain degree.

Recently Darius came up to me, his fogged goggles placed high upon his head and a broad grin and look of pure pride across his face. He declared, "Mom, I have a surprise to show you. Follow me!"

I joined him and his swim instructor, Heather, by the pool. She gave him a knowing glance, and he jumped into the pool, bobbed to the surface, swam his way to the wall, grabbed the edge, and pulled himself up and out. I was ecstatic to see his programmed path to water safety.

The next afternoon found us both in the pool. Feeling confident, Darius told me to watch him swim from the pool steps to where I was wading about ten feet out. He placed his face in the water and pushed off from the steps. About five strokes out, I saw him panic and reach up in the air, flailing in the water. I quickly came to his rescue and pulled him up into my arms. Startled, he sputtered and coughed to regain his breath.

I realized Darius didn't know his own limitations. Although he had learned how to swim back to the edge of the pool—about five strokes—he was not yet prepared to swim about freely.

Darius's water escapade provoked my own thoughts. How many times have I been zealous to do something more, something bigger, and something better than my own limitations allow, and learned lessons the hard way? At times, I defeat myself in my own efforts.

Knowing my own limitations, accepting myself for who I am, and learning and growing steadily in my role as a woman, wife, and mom brings true contentment and achievement.

~ Angel Shahrestani

> *Dear God, thank you for giving me*
> *the strength to do and be all things*
> *pleasing to you (Phil. 4:13).*

Consider it all joy, my brethren,
when you encounter various
trials, knowing that the testing of
your faith produces endurance.
~ James 1:2-3 (NASB)

Pushing through Life's Pain

"I can't do this anymore! Make it stop; it hurts too much!" These were just a couple of the phrases I heard not long ago from a friend who was delivering her baby. I was honored to be asked to be in the delivery room, and the experience was a blessing as well as a learning opportunity.

As a mom, I have often cried out to God with many of the same phrases as my friend during her delivery: "This is too hard; I can't do this anymore." But mine sometimes sound more like, "I cannot spend one more day trapped inside my house because my children are sick" or "I just can't do one more load of someone else's laundry."

I have often wondered why I have to experience pain to experience good things, but it seems that the two go hand in hand. In childbirth, joy and pain are mingled. This same combination of emotions is often present in our everyday struggles. The greatest joy often comes out of our deepest pain. But take heart—your experiences are developing character in you, and that character is what you will use to teach your little ones.

So breathe deeply and push through those difficult times. It may be out of those times that the greatest blessings await you.

~ Melodi Leih

Dear God, in the darkest of times,
show yourself as a light to my child.
Prove to her that you are there.

The hardest of all is learning
to be a well of affection and
not a fountain, to show them that
we love them, not when we feel
like it, but when they do.
~ Nan Fairbrother

Mommy Bumps

Do you remember that commercial from a Super Bowl years ago, that silly one with the image of cowboys with their ropes and horses trying to herd cats as if they were cows? I actually think of that commercial often.

That same image comes to my mind when I am trying to get my five-year-old and two-year-old boys to cooperate in doing something that is on my agenda.

Sometimes it's those simple little tasks that are the most difficult as a mom. Many times I realize that what I think is most important to be doing right now conflicts with what my children think is important. I've heard these moments referred to as "mommy bumps."

When I am able to take a minute and put these "mommy bumps" in perspective, I realize that just maybe my goals of cleaning, grocery shopping, and laundry aren't the most important things to accomplish at this very moment. Although I do get those things done eventually, sometimes it's easier to do the tasks after making time for my children: taking three minutes to read Barney one more time, stopping to comment on a new piece of artwork, or even playing a quick game of hide-and-seek. We shouldn't be at the beck and call of our children all the time, but sometimes when I put my children's agendas first and satisfy their needs, I am able to get my work done with much less frustration. Better yet, we are all much happier.

~ Jill Love

Dear God, help my child to desire you and your ways above the ways of others.

Trust in yourself and you are doomed to disappointment. Trust in your friends and they will die and leave you. Trust in money and you may have it taken away from you. Trust in reputation and some slanderous tongues will blast it. But trust in God and you are never to be confounded in time or eternity. - Dwight Moody

The House Is Moving

Recently, my son discovered the meaning of the word *dizzy*. He acquired this knowledge while spinning around in the middle of our living room floor. With a big smile on his face, he flung his arms out and spun, succumbing to the freedom of this new feeling. He turned around and around (and around again). With every revolution, he would let out a "Whoa, Mom," but still he continued to turn.

Not surprisingly, within a short time, he began to totter and then hit the floor with a thud. As he lay on the floor, he looked up at me, eyes crossed and unable to focus, and said in his child voice, "The house is mooobing!" Within seconds, I joined him on the floor, laughing at this funny concept.

As he was recovering and his eyes were returning to their intended position, I replayed the episode in my mind.

Isn't that how we, as mothers, think of our lives sometimes? We spin out of control, it seems, as we change diapers, wipe noses, go to playgroup, run to preschool, fix peanut butter and jelly sandwiches, and clean the kitchen five times (not to mention all those things we do after lunch). We're often exhausted and irritable, and our brains are swimming with all that is happening around us.

Sometimes I just need to take a break and stop spinning. I sit down and ask God to help me get my eyes (and heart) back to their intended position. My son has to stop spinning and rest to get his equilibrium back, and so do I. How about you? Can you take some time to do the same? Sit down. Pray. Stay for a while . . . and the house will quit moving.

~ Nikki King

Dear God, as my child seeks you,
remind him that he shall not lack any
good thing (Ps. 34:10).

My children . . . have been a
constant joy to me (except on
the days when they weren't).
~ Evelyn Fairbanks

HALT

A whiny day. You know the kind. When everything is met with a whine. "Why do I have to eat my carrots?" "When can we go to town?" "How come I have to pick up my toys?" "I don't wanna!" "I don't need a nap!" "It's miiiiiiiiiine!"

I think I am going to lose my mind! I just want to shout out, "What's the matter with you? Why are you so whiny?" Then I catch a glimpse of myself in the mirror and see myself asking "why" this and "how come" that. What's the matter with me? Now *I'm* whining!

I read once that you should meet whiners head-on with the acronym HALT—Hungry, Angry, Lonely, Tired.

Four conditions that can lead to the whines. Four conditions that can hit the very young, the very old, and the in-between. Four conditions that are often relatively easy to fix.

So the next time you come nose to nose (or knees to nose) with a whiner, think *HALT*, and see if you can put a halt to the whining. My personal favorite for a cure? A nap, of course. If not for the whiner, then for me!

~ Kathy Dye

Dear God, fill my child's heart with a pure joy that can come only from you.

> Once the children were in the
> house the air became more vivid
> and more heated; every object
> in the house grew more alive.
> ~ Emma Goldman

The Lizard's Tale

The calmness of the afternoon was shattered by a loud "Mommy, I forgot!" My sister, Alison, had put her two-year-old son, Blake, down for a nap. Blake was in the process of being potty-trained but often still "forgot" and had accidents. With his outburst, the adventure began.

Alison picked up Blake and put him in the tub, adding "wash everything in Blake's bed" to her mental list of chores for the day. As the warm water poured into the tub and soothed the little boy, my sister realized that Kaleb, her two-week-old son, had woken up from his nap.

Quickly Alison ran in and scooped up the baby, adding another note to her mental list: "Wash everything in Kaleb's bed." She then laid the baby on her bed, pulled off his wet clothes, and grabbed a new diaper. However, she wasn't quite fast enough, so she added a new note to the list: "Change the sheets on my bed."

Another scream sent Alison running, holding Kaleb. "Mommy, there's a lizard in the bathroom!"

Blake was right. The lizard scurried around the bathroom floor, scared by the boy's screams. Alison put Kaleb back in his crib, ran to the kitchen, and grabbed a cup. After an exciting chase, she scooped the lizard into the cup and promptly deposited it outside.

Alison reclaimed the crying baby, hurried back to a still-crying preschooler, and discovered the cause of Blake's new distress. In the excitement of the moment, the lizard's tail had come off and was still lying in the middle of the floor, wiggling. Tears of frustration quickly came to Alison's eyes as she threw the tail in the trash.

"But, Mom, the lizard can't live without his tail," her small son pleaded.

After a short science lesson about lizards, Alison cleaned everyone up for the funeral of the lizard's tail.

A frustrating few moments turned into a lifetime memory and unstoppable laughter at the retelling of "The Lizard's Tale."

Motherhood is a moment-by-moment journey. Some of those moments are calm and enjoyable, while others are frantic and adventuresome. Learn to enjoy each moment, whatever it may bring.

~ Charlotte Packard

> *Dear God, give my child a zeal*
> *for life and a passion to serve*
> *you unconditionally and without*
> *hesitation.*

10

Perspective

Nothing great was ever achieved
without enthusiasm!
~ Ralph Waldo Emerson

A Zest for Life

My oldest son, Andrew, is quiet, has a long attention span, and can keep himself entertained with toys and books for long periods of time. He has always been a very easy child. In fact, I began to think all children were this easy!

Then came Ethan. Ethan is now two and a half . . . and my life and opinions on parenting have been forever changed. Here is an example of a typical "Ethan" situation.

Ethan came running downstairs, proudly announcing "I ate money!" When I asked him what he meant, he told me he had put a coin in his mouth and then swallowed it. I called my doctor and was told to bring Ethan in. While sitting in the waiting room, Ethan convinced an eight-year-old girl to teach him to knit; he got a middle-aged man with poor English to read him a fishing magazine; and after getting an elderly lady's attention by hitting her shoulder, he proudly announced to her the "accomplishment" that brought him to the doctor's office. She replied with a smile, "Honey, spending money is much more fun than eating it!" Later, while waiting for his X-ray, Ethan went up to a man in a short hospital gown and exclaimed, "You have hairy legs—just like my daddy!"

As I watch Ethan, I think about his future with his excitement for life, his willingness to accept everyone, and his high energy level. I wonder what might happen if I focus on the positives of his personality and energy— where he will go and what he will become—rather than try to squelch them. And then I wonder how I can be more like him.

~ Jill Love

Dear God, use the qualities you have given my child to help him reach his greatest potential.

> Because I am a mother, I am
> capable of being shocked, as I
> never was when I was not one.
> ~ Margaret Atwood

Firsts

Our mothering days are filled with so many exciting "firsts." There is that first smile, first step, first word, and first day of school (OK, that one is bittersweet).

I recently experienced a surprise "first" from my eighteen-month-old. I laid her down for her nap on Sunday afternoon and then proceeded to do some straightening up. She seemed a bit restless because I heard her rolling around in the crib, but she wasn't crying or fussing, so I just let her play in bed. She seemed happy, and I thought she would eventually play herself to sleep. Then strange banging sounds started, so I headed in to investigate. Imagine my surprise when I opened the door to find an empty crib and a very disassembled room! No wonder she was so happy. She'd had a great time , especially with the wet wipes. She had taken them out one by one and placed them in every nook and cranny imaginable. Stuffed animal "shrapnel" from the funfest was everywhere! Although the ordeal made more work for me, surprisingly I was able to look at the situation and laugh.

So often I don't realize that my children are just that—children. Sometimes I get frustrated when my children accidentally spill something or are playing too loudly. I am definitely not the mom in the paper towel commercials—you know, the one where the child spills an entire container of juice, and the mother just smiles because she has the right paper towel for the job? My thoughts would run to the fact that three dollars was just spilled on the floor and now I needed to clean it up.

Sometimes I just need to take a breath and be thankful that I have been blessed with little noses to wipe and clothes to fold. Oh, and speaking of "firsts," tonight we have a new one—her first night in a big bed. I will really need to put my words into practice and enjoy this new stage of my daughter's life. After all, how many times will my little Houdini move out of her crib and into a bed?

~ Jennifer Prince

Dear God, develop within my child
the strength to go to you first with all
her joys and struggles.

Few things are more
rewarding than a child's open,
uncalculating devotion.
~ Vera Brittain

Mom, You're an Amazing Cook!

I don't cook—I burn! I even have a reputation for ensuring that macaroni sticks to the bottom of the sauce-pan. So when my daughter Olivia exclaimed one day that the clam chowder and burned English muffin I served in the middle of an eighty-degree day was fabulous, I became curious. What makes a good cook? Is it measuring everything to the last detail, the extra special ingredients you add to the recipe, or perhaps just watching the pan instead of walking away, only to be reminded of it by the hissing as it boils over?

As we giggled over the bowl of soup we shared and swapped muffins to ensure that we both had equally burned bits, I realized that the food was secondary. It was the love we shared over food that had brought us together.

That love that can be spelled out in alphabet soup letters: TIME. How often we forget that it's not the food we may have lovingly prepared or the great trip to Disney World or the new toys or the stylish clothes that matter. What our kids really want and need is our time.

Olivia and I spent the rest of the afternoon making pretzels in the Easy Bake oven, and we savored the salty, yummy, uncooked goo that sort of looked like pretzels. As we spent time measuring and adjusting the recipe, the pretzels started to taste even better—and began to look like they should!

We shared a few hours of laughter and love, and at the end we clinked our milk glasses together, and Olivia said, "Cheers, Mom, to mothers, daughters, friendship, and God. Amen!" Amazing insight from my wise seven-year-old. She will likely be a far better cook than I, but she will treasure most the time we spent together, practicing our cooking.

~ Samantha Mulford-Phillips

> *Dear God, teach my child the value of her time. Remind her of the plague of complacency and laziness.*

An adventure is only an
inconvenience rightly considered.
An inconvenience is an
adventure wrongly considered.
~ G. K. Chesterton

Adventures

A few nights ago, I was sitting around with some friends, and we were all reminiscing about our growing-up years. A couple of the guys in the group started talking about high school sports injuries. You know the kind—broken ribs during a snowmobile accident, a busted foot from a foul in a basketball game, a torn knee from a big football game. As each story was relayed, the amount of pain from the injury increased. What adventures these guys seemed to have had.

In my mind, I tried to count up my sports injuries and came up a little short. The only one I could think of was when, before performing with my dance team at a half-time show in high school, I pinched my cheeks a little too hard. Broken blood vessels in my cheeks created purple, finger-shaped marks. Maybe not the most adventurous wound, but a funny one nevertheless. Adventure is the spice of life and makes things fun and interesting.

Before you tell me that your life has ceased to be adventurous, think about what you do every day. Maybe you wake up at 4:30 a.m. to feed a hungry infant, or perhaps you make three little lunches while dressing for work. Maybe you're the mom who seems to spend all day answering the question "Why?" Sounds like training for a marathon might be easier!

Maybe you haven't broken a rib, a foot, a knee, or even any facial blood vessels recently, but don't underestimate your everyday adventures. Motherhood is an everyday adventure, with little ones bouncing off chairs, running circles around you while you are trying to get the laundry folded, and fearlessly climbing rocks, trees, fences, and anything over a foot high—always inquisitive about the world around them! Take a moment today or this week (or maybe when your children are eighteen and you have a moment to stop) and think about your everyday adventures.

~ Rachel Ryan

Dear God, give me the insight to see the fun in the everyday adventures.

*Rain beats a leopard's skin, but
it does not wash out the spots.*
– Ashanti proverb

Finding Fresh Air

"I am *way* too old for this," I thought as I careened around the corner of the pasture at a brisk canter. It was a fine spring day in Georgia, unusually cool and beautiful. I had seized a rare opportunity while my daughter was at preschool to sneak away to a friend's house and ride my new horse, Blackjack. Despite my nervousness, I felt a thrill that I hadn't felt in years.

Like many moms of young children, I had put aside hobbies when I became a mother. One day when my children were finally out of diapers, I realized, much to my horror, that I didn't have a *single* hobby. Then my friend asked me to come horseback riding with her. I jumped at the chance. I had been a horse-crazy teenager, always looking for opportunities to ride. The ride with my friend that day was exhilarating. With my husband's support, I soon acquired an elderly, somewhat cantankerous mount named Blackjack and started trying to fit riding back into my life.

During those first few rides, I quickly discovered that the teenage girl who loved to ride fast and thought it was fun to be bucked around the pasture was long gone. Instead I had become timid and was fairly obsessed with how much it would hurt to fall on my head. I also struggled with the whole concept of taking "me" time. I felt that I wasn't being productive. But as I spent afternoons taking short rides, I found a part of myself I had stuffed deep down inside. I slowly recovered my confidence, and I began to feel more alive. My husband and children began to see a different, more fun side of me, and these days they often ride with me.

I have learned that moms of young children must take some time to breathe fresh air, perhaps to rekindle those old loves that once gave us such joy. Taking that time will ultimately make us happier, more confident, and more loving mothers.

~ Leigh Ann Falconer

Dear God, help my child embrace the unique interests and talents that you have placed within him.

> There are only two things a
> child will share willingly—
> communicable diseases and his
> mother's age. ~ Benjamin Spock

Mud and All

I just love autumn, when the leaves are falling and I have apples baking in the oven! There's just something about piling on extra clothes and making hot cocoa with marshmallows. So when my son's preschool class met at the farm market to enjoy the fall festivities, I was right there like a "good" mom. Elias is an active boy, not bad per se, but always on the go. Jumping in mud puddles became a fun game, which was fine because I had anticipated that move and put his big rubber boots on. What I hadn't expected was his running at full speed and those boots then sticking in the mud, sending him head over heels like a superstar gymnast into a pondlike mud puddle, which drenched him entirely from head to toe. Once out of the mud, Elias proceeded to drop his muddy drawers and relieve himself inside the opening of a nearby tepee! The gasps of horror told me I wasn't such a good mom after all.

All of those moms were watching me, eyes glaring, as I walked by with a wet, half-naked three-year-old trudging behind me. At the time, I could only shrug. Now I can smile. It was one of those wild and crazy mothering moments—and with a son like Elias, there are many of them.

I have laughed and cried and sometimes questioned if what I'm doing really makes any difference or matters at all. But I know it does matter in so many ways. It matters because I can share these stories with other moms, and I have them in my heart forever. And it matters because I have a vision for my son. One day my son will be a man, and then we will laugh together about how he embarrassed me. These days are precious and will be gone just as quickly as the fall leaves. So I will cherish them and thank God for the treasures of children and the hope he brings . . . and for the gifts of my MOPS friends, who accept us just as we are, mud and all!

~ Noelle Schabel

Dear God, assure my child that you do not expect perfection from him but rather a yielded and obedient heart.

> When it is dark enough,
> men see stars. ~ Ralph Waldo
> Emerson

The Dark

As we often do in the summer, last weekend our family dug out the trusty tent, filled a cooler with food, loaded the car, and headed for the mountains. It was not long before we had set up camp, roasted hot dogs over the campfire, and sat lathered in bug repellent around the warm glow, enjoying the evening.

When we're camping, the dark never fails to amaze me. Living in the city, I forget how dark it gets without the street lamps, neon signs, and night-lights that normally adorn our evenings.

As we sat in the growing shadows of night, wondering just how many bears were lurking between us and the tent, we began to see the stars. As we tilted our heads back and looked up at the night sky, we were awed at the sight. These were the same stars that hovered over our heads every night, but tonight they were able to take center stage in a performance all their own.

It struck me then that just as it takes a dark night to see the stars in all their glory, sometimes it takes a dark night in our lives for us to notice the light that we normally take for granted. When we wake up on the wrong side of the bed, an unexpected compliment from our spouse can go a long way. After a hectic day of struggling with the kids, a heartfelt picture from a little one can be enough to bring a smile. When going through a rough time, we are warmed by a simple hug from a friend.

It is in moments like these that we realize there is light all around us, and we do not have to be afraid of the dark.

~ Jessica Potter

Dear God, may my child lift his eyes to the hills and find help in you. May he know that his help comes from the maker of heaven and earth. Show my child that you will not let his foot slip and that you do not slumber (Ps. 121:1–3).

> Mothers have as powerful an
> influence over the welfare of
> future generations as all other
> earthly causes combined.
> ~ Sir John S. C. Abbott

Reaching Out

Last week I fixed a meal for thirty international students as part of my church's community outreach program. It took almost all day to shop, prepare, cook, and deliver the food. Obviously, this was a significant sacrifice of time, effort, and money for me as a busy mom.

I took my young daughter with me when I delivered the food. Upon our arrival, the hosts looked surprised. It turns out someone else had also been preparing food for the evening!

Needless to say, I was a little frustrated that I had invested so much in preparing a meal that wasn't needed after all. But the hosts were kind, gracious, and grateful, apologizing for the mix-up. Maybe this was God's planning, they said. Since the organizers never knew how many students would attend and since this was the last meeting of the year, it would possibly be a bigger group than normal, which meant they would need all of the food. I left feeling good about my effort.

Several days later, I received a follow-up card apologizing again for the mix-up and thanking me for the meal. Indeed, the group had been extra large that night, and all of the food had been eaten.

Whether we take a meal to a family in need, fill an Operation Christmas Child shoebox for a child overseas, or give our money and time to a worthy cause—whenever we reach beyond ourselves to help others—we model generosity to our children. I want to be known as a generous, giving person. And I want my children to be generous and giving too. We give out of what we have received. It can be hard to reach out to others during this busy season of mothering, but it is so worth it!

~ Janis Kugler

Dear God, help my child to encourage
the timid, to strengthen the weak,
and to be patient with everyone
(1 Thess. 5:14).

> Any adult who spends even
> fifteen minutes with a child
> outdoors finds himself drawn
> back to his own childhood, like
> Alice falling down the rabbit
> hole. ~ Sharon MacLatchie

Rolling Uphill

Autumn is here! The air is crisp and cool, and nature's color palette is warm and inviting. As the seasons change, I am reminded how even the old can seem new again. The mundane can be magical . . . like checking the mail.

Just the other day, my daughter and I decided to spend some time savoring the outdoors while we waited for the mail truck. For me, it was just waiting for another stack of bills to come. But for my five-year-old daughter, it was like she was waiting for Santa

Claus to arrive with a special delivery. She excitedly greeted the mailwoman and hugged the mail as if it were soft and cuddly. I was ready to head inside and start separating the bills from the junk mail. But she had other ideas.

"How about we roll uphill, Mommy?" she asked. *Why not?* I thought. So together we rolled uphill, mail tucked in our shirts, all the way to the front door of our house. I'm sure we were quite a sight for the neighbors. It was a breeze for my daughter's young body, but it wasn't so easy for me. I had a lot more weight to roll up that hill! But I'm glad I took the time on that cool fall day to get a little fresh air and view the mundane in a magical way through my daughter's eyes.

~ Nicole Smith

*Dear God, preserve in my child
the ability to see with awe and
appreciation the world that you've
created.*

11

Celebration

There are no seven wonders
of the world in the eyes of a
child. There are seven million.
~ Walt Streightiff

"Special" Occasions

When I was a child, I loved to look at the towels
in the back of our linen closet. The towels had been

253

wedding gifts for my parents and were fancier and more plush than any we were allowed to use. We were always told that they were to be saved for a "special" occasion.

I recently was visiting my parents' home and came across the towels still neatly folded in the back of the linen closet. Their color has faded, their lace has shriveled, and their softness has been replaced by the stiffness of old material. The towels are worn not from use but from the lack of it. The so-called "special" occasion never came, and now the once-beautiful towels would fit better in the rag bin than they do in the linen closet.

We have each been given this season of mothering to use as we choose. How will you use this precious gift? I am determined to use all moments as they come—the "special" ones and the very ordinary ones. Don't take the moments with your children, your friends, and your loved ones and set them on the back of the shelf. Don't wait until everything is perfect or your house is clean or your children are perfectly behaved—because that moment may never come.

Take each moment and use it up, wear it out, and enjoy it to the fullest. Fill the moments with laughter and love, memories and traditions, and enjoy the gifts you have been given.

~ Charlotte Packard

> *Dear God, use my child for your glory.*
> *Mend her broken places into spots of*
> *strength through which your power*
> *is revealed.*

The most important prayer in
the world is just two words long:
"Thank You." ~ Meister Eckhart

A Child's Thankfulness

My son anticipated his birthday with excitement—
family, friends, party, cake, and gifts. When his birthday
arrived, he had a great time. It was a busy day, full of all
the things kids love.

So that night, when he called me to his room after
he had gone to bed, I was very surprised to find he was
crying. When I asked what was wrong, he told me, "I feel
like I don't appreciate all the stuff I got for my birthday
and all the things I already have. I have enough."

Wow. What a statement from my child! We spent some time discussing how God sometimes blesses us with a lot of things so that we can share what we have with others. We talked about some of the opportunities he has had to share his toys and games with his friends. I also helped him remember how he gave away toys and clothes he did not use anymore to other children who would be helped by his kindness.

Then we talked about the importance of thanking God for giving us so much. It was a special moment of growth for a little boy—and for his mom, who sometimes forgets to be thankful for all she has.

~ Sylvia Reese

Dear God, instill in my child a grateful heart for all that you have done for him.

Love is, above all else, the gift of oneself. ~ Jean Anouilh

Glitter

It's a banned substance from the newly carpeted area of our church, yet you can find it in the bottom of my daughter's backpack. What is it, you ask? Glitter. The quintessential tiny, shiny material for crafting Valentine's cards with wee little hands. You can have piles of red and pink construction paper hearts, doilies, markers, feathers, sequins, and lace trim, but nothing says Valentine's Day like great globs of glue gummed up with glitter. As the glitter is sprinkled or poured from little canisters, you find instant satisfaction in watching your Valentine take on texture, color, and sparkle.

But there's imperfection inherent in crafting with glitter. Poured too extravagantly, some might not catch the glue. Excess glitter is hard to recapture and even harder to vacuum out of carpet. Too much glue takes ages to dry, and too much glitter will fall off projects if handled too roughly. February glitter can lodge itself in dark backpack crevices and reappear in May. And sometimes the artist can wear the art when stray glitter affixes itself to a cheek or a sweater.

In recent years, craft companies have invented glitter glue pens and paints with the glitter mixed right in, tidying up this timeless craft material. But no matter how glitter is dispensed, its appeal lies in its beauty as it catches the light. My daughters recognize this beauty and use glitter with wild abandon, never once giving thought to glitter's untidy qualities. I am learning to revel in the messiness of this beauty on Valentine's Day, and I will delight in watching my daughters' love affair with glitter morph into glitter nail polish and glitter makeup all too soon.

Meanwhile, I am going to shake out my love on my kids like glitter. I want my love to stick in big clumps on my girls, and I want them to find it years later. I want my love to bring a smile to their faces because of its beauty, and I want it to add color and richness to their lives . . . no matter how messy it will get.

~ Rhonda Headley

Dear God, help my child to be so full of your love that it bubbles over into every part of her life.

> Biology is the least of what
> makes someone a mother.
> ~ Oprah Winfrey

Breakfast in Bed

Yesterday morning I woke up extra early to prepare for the event. I dressed for church and then slid back between the sheets, pretending to be fast asleep. The big event? Breakfast in bed. Downstairs my four children chattered away, scrambling eggs, stemming strawberries, and toasting slices of whole wheat bread. It sounded a little crazy down there, but that was because they're not used to making breakfast. The other 364 days of the year, that's one of my jobs.

"Mom, wake up. We've got a surprise for you!" We all pretend I'm surprised, although they have long since figured out I don't sleep in makeup and church clothes. Handmade cards are presented as we sit in the bedroom and enjoy breakfast together. Even though I nag them about clean rooms and punctuality, limit television and computer use, and sometimes serve up the morning cereal with a grumpy 'tude, the sentiments in the cards and my kids' spoken words and actions let me know they appreciate my mothering. They've noticed the filled fruit bins and fresh sheets, noted my cheerleading from the sidelines of their lives, and actually heard a few of the wise words I've offered when they've struggled over an issue.

Mother's Day is over until next year, but my breakfast in bed will carry me through all the other days when it seems none of my children appreciate the daily investments I make into their lives. On those days when my mothering efforts are rewarded with nothing better than an angry glare, I'll savor my Mother's Day memories of scrambled eggs served with a side dish of gratitude and love.

~ Shelly Radic

Dear God, thank you for my child,
today and every day.

She knows how to make virtue
out of necessity. ~ Audre Lorde

I'm Thankful

I'm thankful for spit in the cookie batter. While I don't normally enjoy such an inclusion, I'm aware that I wasn't alone in the mixing and stirring or the licking of the bowl but rather had the help of little fingers and hands!

I'm thankful for paw prints on the hardwood floor. The floor is certainly far from clean, but the prints remind me of the joy and love introduced to our family by our Boxer puppy.

I'm thankful for dishes in the sink. Sure, it would be much nicer if they were rinsed and placed in the dishwasher, but their presence tells me that others feel comfortable in this home as they rummage through the cabinets and fridge, eating and running and returning for more.

I'm thankful for balled-up shirts in the dry cleaner basket. No, I don't relish dropping them off and picking them up, but I cherish the man who thinks highly enough of himself to want his shirts cleaned and pressed and who doesn't care who does it for him.

I'm thankful for a bathtub filled with scented oils, a magazine, and reading glasses. Such lavish innovations allow me to climb in, light a candle, and speak words of thankfulness to God for all these daily things.

~ Elisa Morgan

> *Dear God, help my child to grasp that*
> *your goodness may not always* look
> *good but nevertheless* is *good.*

There has been only one
Christmas– the rest are
anniversaries. ~ W. J. Cameron

You Know You're a Mother of a Preschooler When . . .

Here is a top ten list of how you know you're a mother of a preschooler during the holiday season:

10. The handrail on your stairs is covered in sticky, candy-cane-filmed handprints.
9. You can't find anything in your closet because of the many Christmas presents hidden throughout.
8. In the hands of "helpful" little ones, cookie dough becomes ammunition.

7. Strangely, the bottom half of the Christmas tree is missing its ornaments, just up to where your tot can reach.

6. When confronted with a grumpy store clerk, you immediately respond, "I guess you've had enough Christmas fun; time for a nap!"

5. Groceries are now placed in the backseat to avoid any chance that little eyes might see special Christmas surprises hidden in the trunk.

4. The lights on your Christmas tree are blinking, and they are not self-blinking lights. *(WHY did I plug the Christmas lights into an outlet*

controlled by a light switch that my four-year-old can reach?)

3. You can quote the entire *Mickey's Twice Upon a Christmas* video (including special voices for Mickey Mouse and Donald Duck).

2. The shepherd boy from your Nativity scene is now playing the role of a racecar driver.

1. You hear your three-year-old quote Luke 2 as follows: "And thewe wuh shepuds living out in the field nehby, keeping watch over theiw flocks. Suddenee a miwiad of angels appeawed, pwaising God and saying, "Glowy to God in the highest and on uhth on whom his favo wests."

As you prepare to make memories this holiday season, don't let the flying dough or incessant blinking lights get in your way. From one mother of a preschooler to another, I pray that you will experience God's favor and peace this Christmas season.

~ Cheryl Davis

Dear God, stretch my child's faith
that he might believe more than he
thinks he can.

I sometimes think we expect too
much of Christmas Day. We try to
crowd into it the long arrears of
kindliness and humanity of the
whole year. ~ David Grayson

Christmas Expectations

It's been a holiday tradition for the last decade. My
family gets all dressed up in our Christmas finery and
drives to a friend's house for Christmas Day brunch, which
includes the best cheese grits ever. After praying, we stuff

ourselves silly and enjoy visiting with friends and family. Gifts are exchanged and pictures taken before we head home for a satisfying nap.

Two Christmases ago, however, all the excitement of the morning, combined with the car trip, was too much for my toddler to handle. Shortly after arriving, she got sick all over herself, her older sister, and her father, who was holding her. My daughters' coordinating Christmas outfits and my husband's sweater vest were soaked. The girls wore oversized T-shirts for the rest of the morning, and they were fine with that arrangement. However, after I had spent a half hour calming down a toddler,

washing out her sister's hair, and cleaning up the floor (hardwood, not carpet, thank goodness!), my mood had soured, to say the least.

Our hosts took it all in stride, and most of the guests missed the action completely, so why was I so blue? I was having a hard time adjusting to the situation. I couldn't quite reconcile my expectations for the morning with how things had unfolded. I finally realized I was letting my vision of a perfect family portrait sabotage our day of celebration. No one else cared at all how my family was dressed, just that we were there.

In the end, it would be a Christmas brunch we would always remember, and no harm came to the cheese grits!

~ Rhonda Headley

Dear God, may my child find you present in all the expected and unexpected moments of her days.

270

The happiest moments of my life
have been the few which I have
passed at home in the bosom of
my family. ~ Thomas Jefferson

Christmas Stood Still

"This year, things are going to be different!"

Year after year, I made that passionate vow in November, only to discover in December that things were just the same—things like too much to do in too little time. Shopping, decorating, cooking, wrapping, mailing—all my responsibilities because I assumed Mom was in charge of everyone's Christmas spirit.

Yet our three children—now grown—remember a Christmas that was different, and it has become their favorite Christmas memory. It was the year that our Christmas world stood still.

Snow started to fall early on Christmas Eve morning along the front range of the Rocky Mountains. Soon the wind began to blow, creating an instant blizzard, and within a few hours, the world around us began to shut down. Never mind the shopping wasn't done. Never mind the groceries were not yet in the refrigerator for the traditional feast. Never mind our Christmas Eve church program and other plans. Never mind what was not done.

A magical stillness descended upon our family as two feet of snow piled up around our home, so we created our own candlelight celebration of Jesus's birthday. We made countless snow angels. We stomped around the neighborhood, talking to people we hadn't seen since summer. We absorbed the wonder of this unplanned, God-given gift.

That Christmas, God wrapped our celebration in a magnificent, fluffy white blanket that slowed us down and prepared us to receive his gift of Jesus.

My responsibility as a mom? Only to fully receive the wonder of this unplanned gift. Things were really different that year. And it's my favorite Christmas memory too.

~ Carol Kuykendall

Dear God, help my children to enjoy unexpected surprises in life.

273

Train a child in the way he should
go, and when he is old he will
not turn from it. ~ Proverbs 22:6

Happy Birthday, Jesus

Four little heads bend in worship.

Four sets of hands wield plastic knives sticky with icing, sprinkles, and crushed candy canes, focused on creating a birthday cake fit for a king.

Four young voices debate how many candles should be placed atop the cake. The youngest, just two, has no opinion yet. His mouth is full of candy cane, and he's content to continue shaking sprinkles across the cake top. The oldest, more practical than her sisters, suggests two candles, one for every thousand years since Jesus's birth. The two kindergartners protest, declaring two little candles is not enough to celebrate such an important birth.

That's the opening I look for each Christmas Eve. "Why is Jesus's birthday so important?" I ask.

"He rose from the dead and lives forever, so we keep on celebrating his birthday," the wise big sister replies. This is her tenth year making birthday cakes for Jesus, and she is very certain of her answer.

"Jesus is our Savior, and if we believe in him, we can live forever too!" shares sister number two emphatically. She has been paying close attention the last few years.

"Jesus loves me!" declares the littlest sister, cutting to the heart of the matter.

"Jesus loves me!" their baby brother echoes, just beginning to understand this life-changing truth.

A few hours later, the birthday cake takes center stage on the dinner table, lit with two tall tapers representing with honorable majesty the two millennia since Jesus's birth. A fine compromise to this year's candle debate.

Four grinning mouths, eager for a slice of cake, enthusiastically sing:

Happy birthday, dear Jesus.
Happy birthday to you.

Four little hearts bend to worship.
Worship Christ the newborn King.
~ Shelly Radic

*Dear God, thank you for your special
offering, given over two thousand
years ago, that makes a way for my
child and me to know you personally.*

Contributors

Jill Arnold lives in St. Louis, Missouri, with her husband and two daughters. Proud to be a full-time homemaker, she loves to travel whenever possible. She dreams of being a professional photographer when she "grows up."

Polly Benson, MOPS International area coordinator, is wife to Brian (sixteen years) and mother to three children, Jake, Cassie, and Nathan. She resides in Ohio and is a graduate of Ohio State University. She is passionate about serving MOPS moms and leaders.

Cyndi Bixler is the development events manager at MOPS International. Her married daughter, Lindsey, son-in-law, Jason, and teenage son, Joshua, all bring her much joy. In Cyndi's spare time, she loves playing and teaching piano, helping facilitate recovery of parents in family crisis, and traveling with friends and family.

Paula Brunswick is a MOPS International area coordinator in the Southwest. She has enjoyed encouraging, equipping, and developing MOPS moms for twelve years, serving the past seven years as a field leader. She also serves as a mentor mom at her local MOPS group. Paula lives with her husband, Bob, and two children, Sarah and Ryan, in Flagstaff, Arizona.

Kim Cook currently serves as a MOPS International area coordinator. She lives in Indianapolis, Indiana, with her husband of fourteen years, Gary, and her four children,

Nathan, Tyler, Emma, and Jacob. She is a stay-at-home mom and finds joy in homeschooling her four wonderful pupils at what is affectionately known as the Cook Academy.

Cheryl Davis, vice president of ministry at Stonecroft Ministries, leads efforts to develop effective evangelism models, strengthen volunteer leadership, and guide forty thousand volunteers to share the gospel. With her husband, Dean, she delights in their two children, Elisa and Nathan.

Carla Dietz is a MOPS International area coordinator who is passionate about reaching more moms and families for Christ. She lives in Northern California, where she and her husband, Russ, are blessed to be raising three great boys, Graham, Jason, and Scott.

Kathy Dye lives on a farm west of Alliance, Nebraska. She and her husband, Bart, raise corn, alfalfa, cows, and two kids, Alyssa and Chase. Kathy has been involved with MOPS since 1993, currently serving as an area coordinator for MOPS International.

Jami English was involved in MOPS for many years. She and her husband, Ric, have been married for twenty years and have two sons, Elliott (thirteen) and Grant (nine). The English family resides in southeastern Wisconsin.

Leigh Ann Falconer is a council coordinator for MOPS International. She lives in Thomasville, Georgia, with her husband, Trey, and their children, Austin and Michaela. She and her family spend most of their time outdoors kayaking, horseback riding, and camping.

Beth Flambures lives in Colorado with her husband, Brent, and two boys, Grayson and Jack. After working with MOPS International as the vice president of finance, Beth continues her financial work but has shifted gears, now working with Brent in their family motorcycle dealership.

Carla Foote is the director of media for MOPS International and has responsibility for the magazine, book, and Web publishing functions. She is the editor of *FullFill* magazine (www.FullFill.org). Carla and her husband, Dave, have two children and a half-empty nest.

Kari Glemaker and her husband, Dave, live in a suburb of Cincinnati with their three children, Joshua, Jacob, and Emma. An avid sports fan, Kari has been involved with MOPS for more than ten years and currently serves on staff as a regional coordinator.

Amy Gullion and her husband, Steve, live in Nebraska. She is experiencing an empty nest after raising three children. She loves being a grandma to a precious new grandson. Amy "retired" from being an area coordinator after serving twelve years in field leadership for MOPS International.

Athena Hall lives in Great Falls, Montana, with her husband, Mark, and their six children. She knows the difference MOPS can make and is involved in a teen MOPS group and a MOPS@ group and serves as an area coordinator for MOPS International.

Marcia Hall is joyfully living the life God gave her and hopefully glorifying him through her actions and words. She has been married to her wonderful husband, Rodney, for twenty-nine years and is a passionate mom to her eleven-year-old son, Pierson—the inspiration for many of her "mommy moments."

English major **Rhonda Headley** married her librarian husband more than a decade ago. They live with many beloved books in Cincinnati with their two girls, ages eight and five, who love to read and write as much as their parents do.

Susan Hitts is a MOPS council coordinator in northern Michigan. Through MOPS, she has recently had the opportunity to speak and write on preschool mothering topics. Susan is married to Randy, and together they parent Angela, Teresa, Sarah, Elisa, and David.

Janice Joos is a family manager, a mom to Jonathan and Jacob, a wife to Chris for more than seventeen years, and a breast cancer survivor since 2005. She currently serves as the MOPS council coordinator for northwest central Ohio.

Terri Kearney is the ministry services manager at MOPS International, and she is also a MOPS mentor. Terri lives with her husband, Ken, in Arvada, Colorado. Their daughter, Lindsey, was married in September 2007.

Nikki King lives in Roanoke, Virginia, with her husband of sixteen years and her seven-year-old son. The MOPS "season" of her life, the relationships developed, and the camaraderie felt is something she will always treasure.

When **Lisa L. Knoll** isn't writing, she's living out her God-given roles as a Christian, a woman, a wife to Terry, and a mother to Emily, Julia, and Michael. They live in Wausau, Wisconsin, with Mr. Tumnus, the outdoor cat forced to live indoors.

Janis Kugler is director of organizational messaging for MOPS International. She has a BS in business administration from the University of Northern Colorado and an MBA from the University of Colorado at Denver. She is a Colorado native, is married to her high school sweetheart, Steve, and has two daughters and a great son-in-law.

Carol Kuykendall is a consulting editor and regular columnist for MOPS *MOMSense* magazine, a speaker, and an author of several books, including *What Every Mom Needs* and *Five-Star Families*. She also writes for *Daily Guideposts*. Carol and her husband are parents of three adult children, and Oma and Opa to three grandchildren.

Mary Beth Lagerborg serves as publishing manager at MOPS International. She has written or compiled seven books, including the bestselling *Once-a-Month Cooking* and *Dwelling: Living Fully from the Space You Call Home*. She speaks on topics related to creating a home. She and her husband, Alex, have three adult sons.

Erin Lehmann is a soccer mom who served for fourteen years in MOPS leadership. She lives in southwest Michigan with her husband, Mark, their three boys, and the male dog sneakily picked out when she left for a MOPS convention.

Melodi Leih is a regional coordinator for MOPS International and lives with her husband, Michael, and their three children in California. She enjoys music, scrapbooking, and being with her kids.

Dallas Louis was born and raised in Austin, Texas. (Hook 'em Horns!) She is married to Jeff, and they have three children, Ethan (five), Emma (four), and Elliott (three). Dallas enjoys being a council coordinator for MOPS International, a Bible teacher, a writer, and a speaker for retreats, conferences, and women's events.

Jill Love lives in Oregon with her husband, Steve, and two young sons. After working nine years at Hewlett-Packard and achieving her MBA, she quit her job to become a stay-at-home mom. That's when the real adventure began. . . .

Elisa Morgan has served as CEO of MOPS International since 1989. An author, speaker, and leader, Elisa is married to Evan and is the mother of two grown children and the grandmother of Marcus, who early on labeled her Yia Yia. Elisa also serves as the publisher of *FullFill* magazine, a resource for women of all ages, encouraging them to live out their influence.

Samantha Mulford-Phillips and husband Bruce, along with their two children, Conner and Olivia, live in upstate New York. When she is not hopping around Europe serving as area coordinator for MOPS International there, she can be found ministering to third grade students as an elementary school teacher.

Charlotte Packard and her husband, Mark, have been blessed with three children, Grant, Denae, and Justin. They enjoy life in the Pikes Peak region of Colorado, where Charlotte is a middle school math teacher.

Peggy Ployhar, a wife and homeschooling mother of three, lives in Apple Valley, Minnesota, where she seeks to follow Christ with all of her heart and minister love in truth to a lost and hurting generation.

Jessica Potter lives in Aurora, Colorado, with her husband and young daughter. She has served in various positions with MOPS International and now is a stay-at-home mom. She enjoys hiking, traveling, reading, and being a mom!

Jennifer Prince and her husband, Earl, reside in Virginia, where they are having fun parenting their three children, Aubrey, William, and Hadley. Jennifer has been involved with MOPS for eight years and currently serves as a council coordinator.

Shelly Radic is the director of ministry life at MOPS International. She and her husband, Bruce, are parenting three teenagers and one grad student, all of whom excel at providing interesting material for mothering stories.

Sylvia Reese is a MOPS International area coordinator and has been involved in the ministry of MOPS since 1991. She also is involved in her church's music ministry, teaches piano, and works part-time in the local school district. Sylvia and husband Dale have two sons and live in Pittsburgh, Pennsylvania.

Stephanie Rich is a kid at heart and loves playing with her six-year-old son, Sean. Being a single mom has changed her life and taught her that you can do anything you put your mind to with God's help. When she is not playing, she enjoys her work at MOPS International as marketing manager.

Susan Richardson, her husband, Preston, and their two daughters are long-time Texans. After spending seven years as a MOPS field leader, Susan currently serves as a mentor mom for her home MOPS group. She loves being a mom!

Rachel Ryan is the media manager at MOPS International. When she's not feeding her passion for ministry, she enjoys spending time in the foothills of the Colorado Rocky Mountains with her family, friends, and 130-pound St. Bernard, Molly Brown.

MOPS International acknowledges Rachel for her work on *Mom, You Make It All Better*.

Noelle Schabel celebrates life's battles through mixing humor and reality. In addition to her most important roles of mother and wife, she is a public speaker, writer, and artist. Children Trinity and Elias are barely seventeen months apart, and husband Scott keeps busy as a medical doctor. "God and chocolate bring me through," Noelle often laughs, but speaks with sincerity.

Angel Shahrestani and her husband, Babak, live in Southern California and never find a dull moment in parenting their four sons, Alex, Niko, Cobi, and Darius. Angel is a ministry director at Coast Hills Community Church and has also worked for MOPS International, where she piloted the national Great Moms Walk.

Susie Sims resides in Colorado with her husband, Kendall, and their three daughters, Stacey, Abbey, and Rebecca, who are now in the tween/teen years. Aside from God and her family, her greatest passions are music and writing.

As the Tallahassee area council coordinator for MOPS International, **Nicole Smith** enjoys speaking to local groups as well as writing, volunteering, and working out. She is married to her high school sweetheart, Tim, and they have two children, Chandler (eight) and Corbyn (five).

Miché Tentor is wife to Larry, a mother of two, and a MOPS leader who lives in Glen Allen, Virginia. Her mission is to serve God through serving others, and she has a passion for growing leaders.

Chris Ulshoffer lives in Littleton, Colorado, with her husband, Lee, and their four children. Chris is a mentor mom in the MOPS group at her home church and a controller at MOPS International, where she has been on staff for fourteen years. Chris enjoys spending time with her children and their horses as well as playing piano and reading.

Barbara Vogelgesang and her husband, Jim, are the proud parents of Nick, Libby, Sarah, and Alex. She loves performing around the country with her family or enjoying company in their stone farmhouse in rural Pennsylvania. Barb's passion is bringing families closer to each other and to Christ through her performing, speaking, and writing.

Bethany Wingo is a Florida native transplanted to Colorado. She loves the outdoors, has been married to husband Joey for two years, and works in the leadership development department at MOPS International.

About MOPS

You take care of your children, Mom. Who takes care of you? MOPS International (Mothers of Preschoolers) encourages, equips, and develops mothers of preschoolers to be the best moms they can be.

MOPS is dedicated to the message that "mothering matters" and understands that moms of young children need encouragement during these critical and formative years. Chartered MOPS groups meet in approximately 4,000 churches and Christian ministries throughout the United States and 24 other countries. Each MOPS group helps mothers find friendship and acceptance, provides opportunities for women to develop and practice leadership skills in a group, and promotes spiritual growth. MOPS groups are chartered ministries of local churches and meet at a variety of times and locations: daytime, evenings, and on weekends; in churches, homes, and workplaces.

The MOPPETS program offers a loving, learning experience for children while their moms attend MOPS. Other quality MOPS resources include *MOMSense* magazine, MOPS books available at www.MOPShop.org, website forums, and events.

With 14.3 million mothers of preschoolers in the United States alone, many moms can't attend a MOPS group. However, these moms still need the mothering support that MOPS International can offer! For a small registration fee, any mother of a preschooler can join the MOPS International Membership and receive *MOMSense* magazine (6 times a year), a weekly MOM-E-Mail of encouragement, and other valuable benefits.

Get Connected!

www.MOPS.org

More books for moms

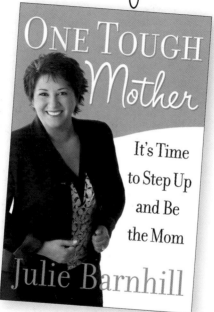

Author and funny lady Julie Barnhill shares ten guilt-free ways to stand firm and be the mom!

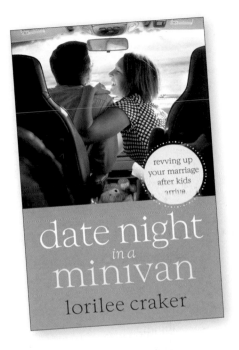

revving up
your marriage
after kids
arrive

date night
in a
minivan

lorilee craker

Full of humor, stories, and road-tested tips, *Date
Night in a Minivan* helps moms deal with the hot-
button issues that surface after kids arrive.

ℛ Revell
a division of Baker Publishing Group
www.revellbooks.com

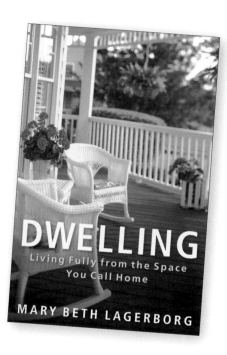

A warm look at the true heart of home—and how
to make yours a place that helps your family rest,
recharge, and go out to face the world.